FINDING MY FEET
Claire Lomas

**Claire Lomas
Books**

FINDING MY FEET by Claire Lomas

Published by: Claire Lomas Books, Melton Mowbray.

**Claire Lomas
Books**

Printed and bound by: CPI Group (UK) Ltd, Croyden. CR0 4YY
Interior Design by: Claire Lomas and Stuart Hall
Cover Design by: Claire Lomas and Stuart Hall
Front Cover Photograph: © PA
Back Cover Main Photograph: Robin Plowman
Back Cover Top Middle Photograph: Nicola Bensley

Paperback: ISBN 978-0-9927990-1-4

Hardback: ISBN 978-0-9927990-0-7

A CIP catalogue record for this book is available from the British Library

First Edition

For Maisie

FOREWORD

That awful moment when the call came to inform us that Claire had had a bad fall at Osberton Horse Trials and would probably never walk again, sticks in my mind as 9/11 does.

This was a talented rider but more over a lovely person. Along with her equally warm and fun mother they had become an integral part of many cross-country clinics I gave. How could this girl live without her driving passion of eventing and horses? How could she?

After an extremely speedy turnaround in comparison to others in her condition, Claire was out of hospital and watching her own two young event horses compete with her mate Lissa - my daughter.

She drove me round the cross-country course in her 4 wheeler. She was very low and our conversation turned to the misery of her new existence and how she was not sure that she really wanted to endure it. We discussed various routes to suicide and she kept reiterating that she did not fancy that one - or that one. Until eventually I said, "Well, I'm afraid you are stuck here then - so we'd better get on with it."

And, as the next 250 pages portray, she did just that - to an unforeseeable and extraordinary degree.

Lucinda Green MBE

ACKNOWLEDGEMENTS

I have so many people to thank. If you are not mentioned in the book, it is not because I have not appreciated you, but because of the sheer number of people who have helped me throughout my journey.

First and foremost, I would like to thank my parents. They helped me through the toughest days of my life; without their love, positivity and support it would be a different story.

Also, to my gorgeous husband whom I bought for only £20 on an internet dating site. He had no idea what he was letting himself in for, but we have shared some of the best times you could ever wish for. We were both lucky to be gifted with the most beautiful gift in the world, Maisie.

A special thanks to Sue, my auntie who has been like a second mum all my life, and is up for whatever I suggest we do next!

Thanks to my old friends who were always there for me when I needed them most; for saying the right things at the right time, making me laugh when I didn't think it was possible and for treating me just the same as I was before my accident.

Thanks to all my new friends who have come into my life since my accident, I hope you will become old friends as we share even more great times.

I would like to express my gratitude to the medics on the day of my accident, and throughout my recovery. Thanks also to the air ambulance who have rescued me twice.

I feel very fortunate to have found an excellent physiotherapist, Kate, whom I have worked with for years. Not only did she help with my rehab but she became a good friend and could cope with me even when I felt at my lowest.

The equestrian world have given me incredible support, and without them much of what I have done would not have been possible. I also thank all my horses who I loved dearly, they gave me years of fun and taught me so much. I learnt the dedication and determination I have needed in the past seven years.

Thanks to Matt Hampson for giving me hope and inspiring me in the early days, and the Matt Hampson Foundation for supporting the marathon.

I'd like to thank Amit Goffer and ReWalk for giving me the opportunity to walk the London Marathon.

I am forever grateful to everyone who has donated and supported my fundraising challenges. Also to all the people who sent letters and emails; helping me after my accident and congratulating me after the marathon.

All the people who walked with me during the marathon, this kept me going and I thank you for this. I was touched by the 18 special people who donated their marathon medals, thanks to Matthew Pinsent and each and everyone of you.

Thanks to my fantastic friends who have helped me with this book. Betty Orme and Sue Smith for encouraging me to pick up the pen and write it myself, and giving me reassurance chapter by chapter. Lucinda Green, Jo Wyeth, Charlie Massey, Gaynor Nash, Emily Goodale, Harriet Davies, Sue Henton and Mum for either editing or proof reading.

A huge thanks to Dan for understanding my appalling handwriting, typing my book and also editing it.

Thanks to Stuart Hall who helped me put the book together, and designed the covers with me.

Finally, thanks to everyone who believed in me through thick and thin, and to the Nicholls Spinal Injury Foundation. I believe in you.

I am grateful to the following for the use of their photographs PA, Kit Houghton, Julia Boggio, Nicola Bensley, Jo Wyeth, MDR Photo – Michael Rogers, Charlie Massey, Robin Plowman, Ian Piper, Amy Bennett, Mark Twittey, Lulu Kyrlacou and Dan Spincer.

1

I heaved my lifeless body into the ugly, cumbersome shower chair and wheeled it towards the corner of my wet room, for what was one of the daily tasks I was trying hard to adapt to. Simply taking a shower was now a huge effort, both physically and mentally.

My eyes looked down at my broken body which, not so many weeks ago, was toned, slim and fit. All I could see was spindly wasted legs that looked fragile and my stomach which was now soft, floppy and protruding. At the same time as the water trickled down my body, tears rolled down my face. Yet again seeing the running water but feeling absolutely nothing, I felt distraught, angry and sad. Then a very strong muscle spasm almost shot me out of the chair. The water flowing down my back had caused this sudden involuntary movement, and I had to I grab hold of the arm-rest to stay in the chair. I found it ironic how I had just spent hours trying to move my legs, and didn't get a flicker of response, yet when I didn't want them to, they did.

All I could think was how I wanted my old body back. If only I could turn back the clock. Could I ever learn to love this useless body I was stuck with? Life felt like a constant struggle. It didn't finish there. I had to get dry and dressed. These were things I had never had to think about, never appreciated being able to do so quickly and easily. But this was my new life, my new challenge. Sink or swim?

Right from childhood, sitting still was just something I never did. At school, friends would discuss what had been on TV, but I didn't watch TV, I was always on the go.

As soon as I could walk I was on ponies and very quickly fell in love with them. My father called it a disease, one that I would not be able to shift easily. Dad worked long hours on our farm in Leicestershire. He was not keen on horses, often saying "all they do is eat your money." Mum however was passionate about riding and enjoyed eventing. I think I caught the disease from her.

Many hours were spent with the ponies. I wasn't taken to shows very often but I did attend pony club camps and go hunting. The real fun however was our pretend shows in the field, and picnic rides where our ponies came back with yoghurt around their mouths. My partner-in-crime was five years older than me, Ashleigh.

Ashleigh was mischievous, and I thought she was pretty cool. Our childhood was happy, full of fun and plenty of trouble. Frequently our rides would be to the local shop to buy sweets, or in some cases cigarettes for Ashleigh. Once they dropped out of my pocket in the shop. I had no idea but the stern shop lady rang my Mum to tell her. By the time we got home Mum was not too pleased, and Ashleigh was not allowed to come over to ride for a while. This wasn't unusual though, and soon enough she was back for more antics.

On another occasion Mum had been out for the day and on her return was alarmed to smell chip fat. "Why can I smell chip fat on these towels?" she shouted. There was no sign of us. We were outside sunbathing with the oil the chips had been fried in, rubbed all over us. Ashleigh said we would tan better and, of course, what my cool friend said was always right.

At Burghley Horse Trials we made a visit to the joke shop where we found some realistic looking smelly dog poo spray. We sprayed it by cars just where the person would get in. Hiding behind a tree we watched and were thoroughly delighted when someone squelched their foot right in it. I think Mum found some of the tricks we got up to quite amusing really, although she didn't always show it.

My parents gave me heaps of opportunities. I participated in many sports including tennis, skiing, and netball; I played the piano and clarinet for a short spell; I went to dancing lessons. However it was clear to see from a young age that my future was going to be riding. I was hooked, whereas my brother, three years older, was always going to follow my father's footsteps. He was soon out on the farm helping Dad.

I went to the local village primary school where I got my parents' hopes up by showing some potential. They started to think they had bred an academic child. I did the entrance exams for Oakham School and Stamford High School. I was offered a place at both- the choice was mine. It was quite a tough decision.

Stamford was an all girls' school. I got on well with boys and would have preferred a mixed sex school. Oakham had Saturday school. Saturday school? I had never heard anything so ridiculous. The decision was made. I had many happy days at Stamford High and lifelong friends were made.

As a young child I suffered from severe stomach pains. As I grew older they were unbearable. The pain was so intense I would be vomiting, up all night and sobbing. I had many visits to the doctors but was always sent home being told it was a stomach migraine or possibly caused by nerves. After numerous agonizing days and nights, I was referred to Leicester Royal Infirmary where they suspected appendicitis. I had surgery that night to remove my appendix. They were alarmed to find it was a perfectly healthy appendix so investigated further. A large cyst the size of an orange was found attached to my right ovary. Both my ovary and the cyst were removed and I was free of the excruciating stomach pains. Mum and Dad were told that it might not be possible for me to have a child which was upsetting news to them. I was oblivious, and aged 13, wasn't too concerned.

To me, the relationship with my pony felt like the strongest bond I could get. I couldn't wait to get back from school for a cuddle with my best friend.

From the age of three I had quite a few ponies in my life but there was a very special one that kickstarted my love of eventing. I was sent this 13.2hh pony, Clive, to get going and sell for a local dealer. He was inexperienced but boy, was he special. We learned together and developed the perfect partnership. There was not a chance I could let him go; I persuaded my mum to buy him. I'd been looking for a bigger pony but Clive was exceptional and if I got a good year or two on him it would be worth it. Together we went on to compete at some big events including the Pony Club Championships and Pony Trials.

I was aged 13 now and eventing had started to be a big part of my life. Eventing consists of three phases. Dressage - my least favourite phase, shows off the training of the horse doing certain movements and lots of circles. This is followed by showjumping. It is very easy to knock the fences down, which I demonstrated well in the coming years. The final phase is the cross-country: the most fun phase, the most dangerous, and with the biggest adrenaline rush.

I think having such a fantastic pony made me keener than ever. I would go to big events like Burghley Horse Trials and dream of competing there.

Another experience that made me hungry to reach the top was a one-off cross-country lesson with six-time Badminton Horse Trials winner Lucinda Green. Lucinda had always been my idol. Aged three I went into a fancy dress competition as Lucinda, so to hear her say such positive and encouraging things about my riding felt like the boost I needed. I started to believe that one day my dream of competing at Burghley would come true.

I managed to combine school work and eventing right up until the time of my GCSEs. I was pleased with my results in both.

Over the next two years I tried to add in having a boyfriend, a fair few rowdy nights out and some waitressing work. To Mum and Dad I had changed overnight. It seemed like I went upstairs as a pony loving kid and came down as a teenager with a drink in one hand and wearing some alarmingly short dresses. I am not sure how they coped.

I found getting served in the pubs under age very exciting, and soon started dating Jonathan. Jonathan was our farrier, and he was five years older than me. My life had changed, I was growing up. I started driving and now felt independent. The consequences were my poor A-level results.

During this time I also did less riding. This was partly due to having such a great time out on the town and being with Jonathan, but also because I'd had a nasty fall at Osberton Horse Trials. My horse got stuck in the fence and we both lost our confidence. Confidence takes ages to build and a few seconds to lose. I think this fall helped make my decision to go to university easier.

I had always thought I should get a degree no matter how much I loved the eventing. It is very difficult to make a career out of horses, and I wanted to have another job. I needed a course that included a large percentage of practical work.

After looking into it for a few months I discovered McTimoney Chiropractic. It was a degree at Westminster University. A country girl was going to hit the big smoke. How was I going to find my way around? I was looking forward to experiencing London, I also knew I would miss Jonathan, my family, and my horses. I was never keen on staying away, home is where I like to be.

I settled in well, although at times I felt like I was in another country. There were very few British people in my halls of residence. I did feel very smug finding my way around the city with my A-Z. Most of the time I did well but on one occasion I ended up the wrong side of London in a bus, no money and late at night. Disaster!

Jonathan would come to stay every other weekend, and I would come home when I could. I was still riding when I came home. I had a lovely easy horse called Rodney Trotter. It is him I thank for getting my confidence back.

I did enjoy the challenge of going to London on my own, and I am so pleased I have had the chance to live in a city that never stops. However, I was not upset to be told my course had problems and we were being diverted to the distance-learning course at Abingdon. We were given compensation and reduced fees, which was pretty brilliant as I preferred the distance-learning course. It meant I would be able to get a job at home to earn some money, do the course and ride. What a perfect outcome.

It was around this time Jonathan and I were going through a rocky patch. He was ready to settle down and there was no way I was. The thought of having kids was not appealing in any way. Jonathan and I did have some fiery arguments but I felt he was my best friend. He had been in my life for four years now, and breaking up was heart wrenching. I missed him more than I could ever have imagined. He was my first love and we had some incredible times together.

I was working part time in the yard, as well as riding my horses at home. I did not want another boyfriend. I did go out on a few dates but didn't want to see any of them again. To be honest I was still missing Jonathan. I decided a couple of months travelling would do me good. The distance-learning McTimoney Chiropractic course had time off in November and December, so I asked a few friends, and Anna was up for it. We went off to Australia for eight weeks.

Anna and I were very different in character and I was worried about how we would get on being together 24/7 for that long. Anna was more of a party animal than me and I had a greater desire to do sporting activities than her. In the eight-week trip, staying in hostels, we didn't have a single disagreement. It was fantastic. I experienced skydiving whilst I was out there, something I really fancied doing. I was lucky enough to do it above the Great Barrier Reef and land on Mission beach.

I don't know why but I love scaring myself to death. Falling at 120 mph through the sky - I was on a natural high for days. The whole trip helped me get over the split up and I was happy to be home.

One of the reasons I was looking forward to getting back home was because I had met someone special just before I left.

It was Chill Out Bob. He was an unruly young horse bred and owned by a local lady named Hazel. Mum had given Hazel a lesson on Bob. She came into the house smiling: "I tell you what, if you play your cards right you could get this horse to event." My eyes lit up.

I had a couple of horses but neither was going to make the top level. One did take me to a level higher than I had done before when we completed a two star event.

I had soon tried Bob cross-country. Hazel's face was beaming. "I am going to get a new outfit for Burghley!" shouted Hazel. He was a machine cross-country. The other two phases were trickier but it is the cross-country that is the most important. I knew it would be easier to train him to do the dressage and show jumping than to turn a wimp of a horse into a brave horse. Maybe that dream would come true one day and I would compete at Burghley. Anyone involved with horses knows that getting a young horse all the way to the top level can take years of training, often with much disappointment on the journey, and an element of luck. Soon there was another addition to my horses.

Gill was a family friend, and a local farmer. Gill had bred a few horses although she was never going to ride them herself. There was one in her field that had not done much at all. She didn't know if he was quite sound. He was a six year old and although he had been sat on, that was about it.

We were not after another horse. We were actually wanting to borrow her lorry for a three day event. She willingly lent it to us but would not let us pay. She just said: "In return just come and have a look at Roland." We promised to have him for two days just to see if he was sound.

I had never met such an enormous, friendly, droopy-lipped horse. He was a 17.2 thoroughbred. I needed step ladders to get on, and a parachute to get off.

There was something unique about Roland. It was his character. He was soon my favourite. Roland loved being around people, was always bullied by other horses, and was the kindest, gentlest horse I had ever met.

Jonathan may have left my life but new four-legged friends were arriving. I was feeling very ambitious and determined with the eventing. It was going to involve hours of hard work, dedication, knocks. I was willing to do whatever it would take. I had two good owners with homebred horses, my goal was to train them and produce two top level horses.

I had always just had a trailer to transport the horses but, as well as keeping Roland, we got Gill's horsebox. It was an old lorry but to me it was paradise. It had a living area where we could make a drink and get changed - a real luxury.

Eventing is a very expensive sport but with Hazel and Gill paying for their own horses it was now possible to have more lessons. Lucinda Green did cross-country clinics in the springtime, so I could take all four horses. It was one of the highlights of my year; I really looked forward to it. Lucinda became a firm friend, a huge inspiration and a brilliant trainer.

I was still going to the McTimoney College of Chiropractic one weekend a month, and studying from home. I did the minimum work required, and the only thing that made the weekends bearable was my friend Selena. There would be many lectures where we would have the eventing magazine in front of us to read the latest news and results. It was only two days once a month, but if at all possible I would get a friend to sign me out at the end of the day, when I had escaped early.

I enjoyed the practical sessions but lectures just were not for me. The final year was spent in a clinic, treating patients, and it is then I realised why I had stuck with the course. It was easy to see how effective the treatment was and the feedback from patients was usually very rewarding.

I only just scraped through but I passed the course. How many patients would ask what percentage I got in my exams? No one ever did, so I could not see that it mattered at all. It was all about making my patients better.

As soon as I was qualified, Mum and Dad helped me set up a clinic room in their house. It took a while but I started to build up my own little practice. It was always reassuring to know I had my degree in chiropractic, and combining this with eventing worked well. I think even now my friends find it alarming that I could use the title 'Doctor'. It was not only them it surprised, it certainly surprised me as well.

As Bob and Roland moved up the levels in eventing, they gave me so much fun. Bob still lived with Hazel and she would bring him to me three or four times a week to ride. This worked well for us both although I think it would have been easier to have him at home once he reached a high level. Bob's weak phase was the show jumping, and poles frequently fell to the floor, but his cross-country remained his strength. I saw our chances of reaching the Burghley Horse Trials as a possibility.

No other owner in the world was like Gill. She certainly loved her horses but she did not know much about riding, especially not eventing. She very much left decisions to me, was very generous, and above all highly amusing.

I remember Roland's first event where he was misbehaving and napping across the dressage field. Gill looked impressed: "Wow, is that the fancy dressage stuff – that sideways trotting?"

It was wonderful having Gill as part of our team. There was no pressure from her, and as long as she got her bacon butty when we got to the event, she was happy.

Hazel had ridden herself, but was also a good owner. She had two young children as well as a couple of horses, so she had help with them all from her friend Sue. Sue would bring Bob over for me to ride, and she always 'produced' him beautifully for events.

I had been single for three years and it had done me the world of good. I was keeping my eye out for a potential boyfriend. I had got to know Tim from hunting with the Quorn, and also saw him at some events. He was incredibly shy but when I got chatting to him I wanted to get to know him. It took a while but he did eventually ask me out. Tim seemed laid-back and easy-going, quite different to Jonathan. The relationship developed, and I am not sure I ever saw him as Mr. Right but I enjoyed being with him. I did not really want a man who worked with horses, but there was something that I liked about Tim.

In 2004, I was riding a young horse at a cross-country course in Nottinghamshire. It was just a practice before a novice event. She was backing off a fence which had a ditch under so I rode her strongly; this resulted in the worst fall I had ever had.

It was a slow rotational fall and the horse could so easily have squashed me. Luckily she landed on my pelvis rather than my chest or head. I felt like I had ages to move out of the way but there just wasn't enough time. I remember thinking, 'This could kill me'.

As soon as the horse rolled over me I tried to move my toes. I could move and I felt the relief. I soon jumped up not knowing the damage I'd actually sustained. I was mortified when I realised my front teeth had been knocked out. An expensive day! I was airlifted to the Queens Medical in Nottingham; I had fractures to my ribs and pelvis. I had one night in the hospital. I hardly slept it was so noisy. Even after just one night I was pleased to be home.

I was supposed to be on crutches for a month. I withdrew my horses from the upcoming events and felt very sorry for myself. It was tough resting, and I got really fed up at times. The event season had only just started, so my plans had been ruined; I felt gutted.

I managed to take it easy for three weeks until a night out at a Quorn Hunt party. I was always keen to get on the dance floor. With the help of a few drinks I decided I didn't need the crutches and I danced the night away. When I woke up the next morning I looked at the crutches. It felt wrong to use them after the night before so I cautiously walked across the room and I seemed fine. That day I started riding again.

Events were entered and I decided to slowly start building up again. I was using the cross-trainer at the gym as it did not have as severe an impact as running.

I went for my next checkup at the hospital, back on crutches so I didn't get into trouble. After a two hour wait I was called in. "So Claire, you must be off the crutches now?" I was sitting down in the room and must surely have looked surprised: "Well yes, I am," I said. He then continued: "So how is your ankle doing?" I looked at him blankly. "Oh, wrong x-ray," he said as he got the correct x-ray out, " it's your pelvis then?" He looked up at me: "You are still on crutches then?" Awkwardly, I tried to make out that I was. He told me: "Another month on them." Not a chance! I was competing at the Windsor three day event in three weeks' time. I used the crutches to leave the room, and then jumped in the car to get back to ride.

My confidence was bound to be affected by such a horrific fall but I was determined not to let it. It was helped by riding Bob at my first event back. He always made the cross-country feel easy. I was soon back in form, and the fall was just a distant memory.

Both Bob and Roland had progressed to advanced level now, although it was hard to compete for a high placing because of Bob's showjumping being below par and Roland's dressage leaving something to be desired. We had done it on a budget with limited lessons. I had put the hours in, and I felt quite proud of my boys. It was so rewarding knowing I had produced them to that level. Life was good!

I was 26 when Tim and I started to rent my aunt's farmhouse; the house I was actually born in. It had taken a while to get Tim to do this. He was quite happy living with his parents. We had been together for two years and I felt strongly that we should be moving forwards. Tim went along with it but I was the one who had the enthusiasm to do it.

It was a large old farmhouse; cool in the summer and freezing all winter. We couldn't afford to whack the heating on, it would cost a fortune. I loved the place though, and had some great memories of it as a child.

My chiropractic clinic was ticking along. More importantly, I was living my dream. I was competing at the 4-star International Burghley Horse Trials - the event I had visited yearly as a child. Bob was now 10 years old and we had qualified for the highest level competition in the sport. I was now a competitor; how magical this felt.

The morning before we set off to Burghley Park, which was at the back of where I spent eight years at school in Stamford, we thought disaster had struck. Bob had never been lame but when we noticed some swelling in his leg my heart sank. We took him to the vets to have it scanned. I was shaking and started to cry expecting to hear the bad news. To my delight the vet smiled and said, "You can go to Burghley." Hazel, Sue, Mum and I all sighed, and a sense of relief and excitement kicked in again.

By the time I got there I was exhausted, having experienced so many emotions in such a short space of time, but it was truly magical.

Gill's horsebox, a luxury to me, looked out of place. Hazel joked, "We look like the gypsies." There were some really impressive lorries parked up. Many had sides that came out to make even more room in the living area. Hazel was in her caravan, again basic, but it did the job.

So there we were with Bob, whom I had spent five years training to get to this event. We spent the evening laughing about our journey to the four-star event, from the moment I named Bob 'Chill out Bob' to the time we were impressed by his bravery across the country, and Hazel joking about a new outfit for Burghley.

One of the wonderful things about eventing is the places you get to visit. A stunning venue added to the thrill of competing there. I hacked Bob around absorbing it all. You could not get better than this, I was tingling with excitement and my stomach churned with nerves.

Of course a three day event was a serious competition, but to my team and me it was always about how much fun we could have too. After all, that is why we had invested so much time and money into it.

I had some fantastic lessons from my dressage trainer, Judy Bradwell, and Bob produced a test we were absolutely thrilled with. We celebrated that evening with a few drinks in Burghley House. My good friend

Shane, who was usually with me at important events, stayed for the week. We laughed so much at times that we cried. I had to pinch myself several times during the week to see if this was all a dream.

Lucinda did one of her excellent course walks with me. As always she left me feeling positive and confident. I felt ready to tackle one of the most challenging courses in the world. I totally believed in Bob's ability.

I slept well the night before, ate a good breakfast, walked the course again and watched a few early competitors. My nerves kicked in but I had been desperate for this for years, I had lived for this moment.

The warm-up was a disaster. I felt flustered, Bob pulled hard and today, of all days, he objected to a new noseband that we'd tried at his last event which had helped. This caused my warm-up to be far from perfect. There were just a few good practice jumps before we set off.

The main arena was early on in the course and it felt surreal galloping and jumping through it. Shortly after, disaster struck. Bob was never usually distracted but I think a combination of the crowds and a poor warm-up had caused him to lose his focus. We had a stop at the mushroom fence, where the bottom of my stirrup iron dropped out. That was my Burghley over! Riding the whole course with just one stirrup can be done by Mark Todd, but sadly not me.

It was mortifying walking Bob back to the stables. It felt like the world had come crashing down. Well, that is what I thought at the time. Little did I know.

It took a few days to bounce back, and I soon hatched new plans. Back at home I had a few talented young horses, and only four days after Burghley one of them got my spirits back up by winning a pre-novice event. These young horses were much better in the other phases than Bob and Roland so if they went on to the top level they could well be horses that would be in the placings.

Burghley did not go to plan, but I knew we were capable. I was going to put it behind me as a learning experience and come out the next year and give it another shot.

The following Spring showed that Bob's cross-country was as brilliant as ever, Roland was in good form, and the youngsters were very exciting prospects. Life was good. I had dreams and nothing was going to stop me, or was it?

2

With the promising start to the 2007 season I decided to enter Bob and Roland at Bramham Horse Trials, which is one level below Burghley. Both horses had competed there before and had given me good rides. Burghley was my goal in the autumn with Bob.

My penultimate run for Roland was at Osberton Horse Trials. I also took my novice ride, Maddy. She was a striking young grey mare, also bred and owned by Gill. It was the same weekend as the Badminton Horse Trials and luckily I wasn't competing until the Sunday, so I watched all the action there on the TV between riding and getting ready for Osberton. I would have loved to have been there on Bob but it is so competitive to get accepted, and it didn't seem a bad idea to wait another few months before we tackled that top level again.

On the Sunday we had an early start and set off to the event. We were about halfway there when we needed to fill up with fuel. Mum was driving the lorry and nipped out to fill it up. When we hopped back in to drive off, it wouldn't start. We all looked at each other in desperation. Mum tried again but nothing happened. We belonged to a lorry breakdown company, which we rang and they came out. They already knew us and we certainly got our money's worth.

I wasn't sure if we would make the event and, if we did, we were going to be late. I called the organisers and they were great about it, saying they would slot me in once I arrived.

Although I was a bit annoyed that we might miss the event, I was also very hopeful that a new lorry was about to be bought by Gill. She had been on about it for a while, when she said: "Well, this is it, let's start looking for a new box." I couldn't help a broad smile appearing across my face.

After about an hour of waiting, the mechanic pulled up next to our lorry. It was the starter motor and it wasn't long before we were back on our way. Once we got there everything was bound to be rushed. I ran the cross-country course; I was recovering from a nasty cold and it felt great to clear my chest. Then the obligatory trip to the loo before I got on Maddy, whom Mum had ready for me. I did all three phases on her with little time between, and was thrilled with her performance. I was so glad we had managed to get there.

By then it was time for Roland's dressage. Roland understood dressage less than me, and you really do need them to show off. Roland did the opposite; he didn't want to be noticed at all. He was a big horse to get around the dressage arena, and he wanted to get out and do the proper bit, the jumping. This sometimes made him look lame as, due to his antics, he would lose both his balance and rhythm. On this occasion the judge pulled us up. When he realised there was nothing wrong - we were just crap at dressage, I was allowed to continue. I'd had this judge say the same thing before but no one else ever had. I saw Ian Woodhead, who had been training Roland and me, and he reassured me. I put it to the back of my mind.

Roland was a fantastic jumper. Today, he was like a springy ball in the show jumping arena. It was easy to feel his relief and happiness to see a fence. We had done this event the previous year when, in fact, he had done a lovely double clear and been placed. It wasn't particularly tough for him, really I was just using it to improve his fitness before Bramham.

We'd had a dry spring and I wasn't sure if I should run him cross-country. The ground was firm, but it was better than most because it was sandy in the woodland.

Mum said: "Remember you will have to take him to the gallops tomorrow if you don't." "Good point. Right, let's tack him up and I'll just take him steady," was my response.

Before I got on him, I went to the prize giving as Maddy had come second; she had just upgraded to Intermediate level, after a few good results. I had high hopes for her. She was tricky in some ways, but we had formed an understanding of each other. We had a great partnership which is what eventing is all about.

As usual a few nerves kicked in before Roland and I set off, but this was not an important event for us. Roland was going well, we were enjoying our favourite phase. There was a difficult combination fence early on, and once again, Roland impressed me with his ability to fit in neat little strides, even though he was a monster of a horse. He was brave and strong but also liked to check out what he was jumping. He was careful. I was nearing the end of the course. I jumped a fence similar to the one where I'd had my rotational fall three years before, and galloped along the woodland track. I remember very little about what happened next.

What I do remember vividly is lying at the bottom of the tree knowing I was paralysed, a word that I'd hate to hear for a very long time.

Where the woodland track split into two, Roland and I had a misunderstanding; he clipped his shoulder on the tree and catapulted me into it. I hit it with enough force to remove the bark. I couldn't get up. I tried to move but nothing happened. I couldn't feel the ground at all. My body had died but I was very much alive. I was horribly scared.

Roland was caught by another rider who was walking the course, and the competition was held. It took a long time to re-start, as they didn't want to move me until they had the spinal board so that I was lying totally flat.

"What pain level Claire, on a scale of 1 to 10?" asked the paramedic. "9.25," I replied.

It was a fairly precise answer I gave. I do not remember the pain, but what I can remember is the total fear, the numbness externally and internally, and just knowing what I had done. I didn't need a doctor to tell me I was paralysed, there is nothing like it in the world. My life was over, at least as I had known it.

I had to wait a long time for the air ambulance. This was essential because it is a smoother journey and with a suspected spinal injury there must be as little movement as possible.

It was another trip to the Queen's Medical Centre in Nottingham. I have no memory of the flight at all. My poor Mum by this time had rung Dad and Sue, my aunt. Both got straight in the car and were at Osberton in no time. Sue drove the horsebox home with Gill and, of course, Roland who was absolutely fine.

Mum and Dad drove to the hospital in silence, worrying all the way but hoping it was not as bad as it seemed.

That split second had changed my life forever. I don't remember the long wait, I don't remember flirting with the paramedics but there are a couple memories from that day that have stuck with me. One is the sensation of running and the ease of moving, possibly for the last ever time. Bizarrely, the second is going to the portaloo and having a wee. Did I appreciate that? No – why should I? Everyone needs a wee and nips to the loo, don't they?

I do not recall arriving at the Queen's Medical, or the scans and x-rays they did. I had really battered myself this time. I was diagnosed with a fracture to my C7 vertebra, dislocation to T4/5, fractured ribs and a punctured lung.

I vaguely remember the doctor discussing the pros and cons of operating on me that evening. There was a risk they would start and not be able to complete the surgery due to too much bleeding from the trauma. We decided to go ahead.

Titanium rods were inserted into my spine where the dislocation was. It was a long operation, about 7 hours. Of course those who were suffering the most were my parents. They were in a quiet room all night, with just a couple of chairs and a box of tissues; nothing else. Every minute felt like a month whilst they waited for news.

Everything went well with the surgery, but the damage to my spinal cord was severe. Because of the swelling, it was hard to tell the extent of the injury. Over the next few weeks this would reduce and, possibly, I'd regain some movement and feeling. At that moment I was paralysed from the chest down, diagnosed as having a T4 complete spinal cord injury. This means that the injury I had sustained, to the 4th thoracic vertebra, had seriously damaged the spinal cord. I had no movement or sensation from that vertebra down. Luckily the fracture to my neck did not cause any damage to the spinal cord otherwise it would have been a different story entirely.

I started to wake up and it wasn't long before the doctor came in to break the news to me. "It is highly unlikely you will ever walk again," were the words he said. They came as no surprise to me. "Well, you don't know who you are dealing with," I responded. "I was supposed to be on crutches for two months when I broke my pelvis, and after three weeks I was riding."

Being a chiropractor, I knew the extent of my injuries. I also knew that if will power, hard work, and determination could get me on my feet, then I would do

21

it. I wasn't going to sit back and accept this, I was going to fight and give it my all.

I was in the intensive care ward and I was asleep most of the time, quite unaware of anything going on. Mum and Dad were with me at every opportunity. I made sure, when I was awake, that I was as cheerful as possible to ease their pain. It couldn't have been easy. I had been there days when I started to really struggle with my breathing, as I now had pneumonia to add to the other list of problems. The nurse put an oxygen mask on me. I felt like she was trying to kill me, it seemed as if breathing was impossible with this thing on. I flung it off a few times; that resulted in a good telling off from the scary, bossy nurse. "You will end up having a tracheotomy if you don't wear it," she said in a stern voice. Being me, I didn't think I needed the revolting oxygen mask on, I was fine.

I had regular visits from Mum, Dad, Sue and Tim. I had not cried at all. I was being brave, although inside I felt very scared, absolutely petrified. My body felt battered, well the bits I could feel did. The rest felt dead. Two thirds of me was dead. My breathing was getting worse and I was put on a ventilator. They could soon see that I was going to be on it a long time so they had to do a tracheotomy.

I think being asleep, and unaware of this terrifying procedure going on, was the best thing for me. Again, it was my family who suffered most at this time.

Over the next few days I became extremely ill. My temperature was high, I had tubes everywhere: catheter, tracheotomy, chest drain, a drip, and a feeding tube. Mum and Dad visited but I felt too ill to see anyone else.

Being so poorly did mean I was not thinking about what was lying ahead of me. I was just out of it most of the time, and when I was awake I was busy being either sick or feeling unbelievably uncomfortable.

A few days passed. I do not remember these few days but I recall waking up at 4:30 am thinking it was daytime. I asked the doctor where Mum and Dad were, feeling really quite annoyed no one had bothered to visit for a few days. She explained it was 4:30 am and I had had visitors all day each and every day. I went back to sleep feeling a little confused but reassured.

Cards and letters had started to flood in, and I had them all around my bed. The morphine made me hallucinate. There was one card in particular that had a dog on it. This dog would change into a gremlin and jump out of the card into the room. It felt so real and so strange. Not surprisingly, I was really scared.

As my temperature went down and I felt marginally better, I found it frustrating having a tracheotomy. It meant I couldn't talk. Anyone knowing me would understand this torture. It also caused some laughs, mostly when Sue was trying to guess what I was trying to say. One of my questions, as I was starting to feel a bit better, was; "How is Roland?" I was worried he might be hurt. I just looked at Mum and made a droopy lipped face. She knew exactly what I meant, and told me he was missing me and was absolutely fine. He was in fact not missing me and was having a lovely rest in the field.

I started to have physiotherapy. This was to get the mucus shifted off my chest. I was told that the physio would be with me soon. I was in for a really uplifting surprise; he was totally gorgeous. I wasn't looking at my best but he did improve my spirits.

It took a long time before there were any tears. I was in shock. My best friend, Shane, caused me to shed my first tears. It was when I read his card. He wrote such kind words that I was overwhelmed. This happened quite frequently when Mum gave me all the letters and cards to read each day. More often than not it was these that made me cry but they also they kept me going, kept me fighting. Now I was aware of everything, the tough time began. I couldn't speak but I could think. If I wasn't asleep I was thinking about the future that lay ahead of me. Why did I have to survive this but be so broken? My legs lay there like dead weights, and when nurses moved them I could see their hands touching me but it was as if they were someone else's legs. What didn't I worry about? My head was filled with thoughts. How would Tim cope with a girlfriend in a wheelchair? Could I have children? How would I go to the loo? How long might I have to be in hospital? My mind didn't stop working, yet I couldn't talk to people about it.

The intensive care ward was something special. The nurses were becoming friends and the care was first class.

I was starting to get the strength to write to communicate although it looked like a five year-old's writing. Mum and Dad were there and I was trying to say something, so they handed me the paper and pen. I wrote: "I am pissed off!" Quite simple really, short and to the point, but it said it all.

I think we all knew it was going to be a long, hard, road ahead. I loved home, and the prospect of months in hospital was about the worse thing I could ever face.

The nursing staff were so kind to me, even washing my hair whilst I was lying in bed in the ITU. They did everything they could to make me feel as good as possible. It had now been 12 days and I hadn't had a drink. My throat was excruciatingly dry but all I was allowed were little sponges with water or juice on to dab on my tongue, due to the tracheotomy.

I had 12 days in intensive care being spoilt, with two lovely nurses with me all the time, but it was now time to be transferred to Sheffield Northern General. This hospital had a specialist spinal unit, where I would be able to do my rehabilitation. I had not dared ask anyone yet how long I would be in hospital. I couldn't deal with knowing things like this yet.

Now I was at Sheffield, I was 90 miles from home. Was I going to be lonely? This went through my mind so many times. Nottingham was much closer for my family to visit. Some days, whilst I was in the Queen's Medical, they had been in three times. Tim had made a fair few visits there, but he wasn't keen on driving to Sheffield alone.

I was upset at leaving Nottingham. I had got to know the nurses a little and felt secure there. This move was a big ordeal for me.

I was greeted by two friendly and slightly daft nurses, Katie and Mandy. They made me feel better and not only stopped me crying but also managed to get me smiling again.

I was in a ward with two others, both on ventilators. They had neck injuries, and were unable to move their arms. I instantly felt lucky. My arms still worked. I could so easily have been one of them; their injuries made mine look like a scratch.

Adapting to the spinal unit took some doing. I no longer had two nurses to myself. If I wanted something I might have to wait a long time. I did find a very naughty but successful way of getting them over quickly. I could pull the connection on the ventilator off so it would beep. The nurse then came quickly to put it back and I would say: "Whilst you are here can you pass my drink please?" or whatever I needed at the time. Sometimes it was just to move me so I could be comfortable. It felt horrendous having to rely on someone else to move me until I saw the guy next to me ask the nurse to scratch an itch on his face, or wipe his tears away.

I couldn't sleep well at night. My bay was next to the nurses' station. They would chat away, lights seemed bright and the ventilators were noisy. This made a good night's sleep impossible.

One of the special moments came when they put a cap on my tracheotomy. This meant I could speak with a squeaky, silly, voice but I was thrilled to be able to talk again, and I was allowed my mobile phone in the spinal unit. This was a real novelty as I had been disconnected from all my friends for two whole weeks.

I rang Selena straight away. We spoke so often normally, it had been strange not to. She sounded a little surprised it was me. We had a ten minute chat, and it certainly brought a smile to my face. Selena had been someone I would confide in with any problem I was having. At the end of the phone call I said to Selena: "I will be OK won't I? Will I be OK? Maybe I should have died." She said with absolute positivity, and I knew she meant it; "Of course you will darling."

I gradually made my way through a long list of people to call. I loved hearing my friends' voices, and times when I felt alone were made easier by being able to chat.

The most difficult time of the day was the morning. The sleep I got during the night was spent dreaming. Dreams of nights out dancing, events, having fun and quality times with friends were vivid and so powerful. Then, on waking up, tears would well up in my eyes and roll down my face. I would think: 'This can't be my life. This can't be real.' It was the absolute opposite to having a nightmare and waking up to find that everything was fine. My dreams were about the life I'd had, the life I still wanted, but I would wake up to the nightmare that was now the reality. It took all my strength to pull myself together to face the day ahead.

The nurse would soon be in to see me and morning jobs would be done. This included a bed bath and emptying your bowel. I couldn't feel them emptying my bowel, but that was almost worse. I would lie there feeling so disconnected to my body, my dignity had gone and I had no control. "This may feel uncomfortable," said the nurse. I just wished it did. I couldn't feel a thing. The hopelessness was overwhelming, as was the despair; I was so very frightened about my future.

Then once a week it was the ward round. The doctors would visit me and see how I was getting on. I only asked the question I desperately needed to know the answer to. "How long will I likely have to stay here?" I was told around six months. That would mean I would not be discharged until September. Not a chance! I didn't have much to say to that answer.

The mucus on my chest was thick and I couldn't cough it up without help. I would have a physiotherapy session every day. I would be shaken and my chest smacked to try to loosen it. I could then have suction; this was awful to see for my visitors. They would remove my cap and poke a tube down my throat. This would make me gag and then the mucus would be sucked up. I saw it as getting better, removing some of the badness. I had a real feeling of satisfaction and felt a clearer chest after it was all over.

The time had come for me to have the feeding tube removed; this was one of the most unpleasant experiences I had. It seemed to take ages as the nurse pulled the long tube out of my nose. It felt like it was being pulled through the middle of my head, it was disgusting. Even worse than this, I now had to endure weeks of horrid, unappetizing hospital food. They couldn't even make a sandwich tasty; the bread was like cardboard and had hardly any filling. It certainly did nothing to tempt me to get eating again.

I was disgusted to hear that the daily allowance per patient in a hospital is less than in a prison. Some things are just completely upside down and totally wrong.

As Mum visited me every day, she was fabulous at bringing me decent food to try to get me eating again. It took a while to get an appetite; in fact it was never great in the hospital.

Mum also bought me a diary so that I could write down when I had visitors. I often had three a day. This made the difference to me coping or withdrawing into self-pity. My family and friends were capable of making me laugh even when I was at my lowest.

I did wonder why some of the nursing staff chose nursing as their career. There was a handful of caring people but, worryingly, a lot weren't. Some were quite cruel. Maybe they get so used to seeing newly paralysed patients that they forget what the individual is going through, and become hardened to it.

After a week in the ventilator ward, I was weaned off it. This was a process done gradually over a number of days. I had a few hours a day without it, until I could manage all day with the ventilator only at night. Once they could see I was breathing well enough, I had it removed. This was another painful procedure, as they pulled it out of my throat. The only good thing was, it was quickly over. All I could tell myself was that these horrible things were a necessary step in the right direction. I was on the mend.

The doctors at Sheffield Northern General did a fantastic job helping me to get better so quickly. I have always been grateful to them for this. To make a fairly quick recovery was a real boost mentally.

Removing the tracheotomy left a hole in my throat. They taped it over and explained how it would heal naturally. The next day when I was taken for a shower, the plaster had come off a little and some water seeped down the hole in my throat. I started choking as if I was dying. I knew I was alright but the young nurse panicked. "Help, help!" she cried. A more senior nurse came to the rescue. It didn't worry me, but it did make me feel out of control again. I relied on all these nurses for the most basic routine jobs.

I had to face all these chores each day. Gradually, I would start to do more of them myself. Some moments I still laughed, joked and smiled like nothing was wrong, minutes later I could sob and feel pain like I had never felt before. This was not physical pain, it was the mental torture.

Every second of every day I was awake, my legs felt bent and I would try to push them straight, only to then look under the bed cover and see that they already were. I felt like I was riding. I did wonder if I was really going mad now, and it was one of the few questions I asked the doctor. The last position my brain remembers before the spinal cord damage was sitting on Roland. It is common for motorcyclists who suffer motorbike accidents, and horse riders, to spend quite a long time feeling like they are still in that position. It was very strange to feel convinced your legs are in one position and, when you look, to see they are nothing like how you thought.

There were still things that needed to be discussed; one of these being what would happen to my six horses. Only six months before my accident we had bought two youngsters. I got to do only one event on them, two days before my accident. These were now for sale; I had no option. That seemed devastating but I hadn't had the chance to grow as fond of them as Bob and Roland. Maddy and Roland went back to Gill and she just turned them out until we could discuss, at a later date, what we wanted to do. Bart, to whom I did feel very attached, went back to his owner to be sold.

Whilst I was in intensive care, Hazel had been to see Mum to tell her Jeanette, a former Olympic rider and her trainer, had been in touch after hearing about my fall. She would like to take the ride on Bob. This was the last thing on my Mum's mind whilst I was so seriously ill. By the time I got to discuss the horses with Mum, Bob had already been with his new rider for a week or so. I felt gutted. I thought of Hazel as a friend and was sad that I had no input on Bob's future after spending five years training him and getting him to advanced level. I knew Jeanette, who had taken the ride on Bob, but she hadn't been in touch with me at all. She was possibly embarrassed? Maybe she didn't know what to say to me. I chose not to dwell on it, and put it to the back of my mind. I had received over 400 cards and emails, some very kind words from people I knew and also some from complete strangers. This helped to make up for the upset I felt at the loss of Bob.

The swelling in my spinal cord would be reducing now. The first six weeks after a spinal injury is the time you are most likely to regain function. There wasn't a day that went by when I didn't try to move my legs, looking at them and willing them to just show a twinge of movement. I had got burning and tingling sensations in my legs all the time, we were all excited that this was the start of improvements. We would try to stimulate feeling by squeezing the feet, and Mum would spend a long time moving my legs.

I was sending the strongest signals from my brain to my legs, but when it got to T4 (chest) level it was cut off instantly. There was nothing I could do about it – except to keep trying.

After two weeks lying flat, I could start to sit up. This had to be gradual though. I soon discovered why. When I started to sit up my blood pressure dropped making me feel very sick. So over the next fortnight I gradually got used to sitting up, slightly higher each day.

I was delighted to hear the doctors tell me I could now start to be hoisted into the wheelchair and get mobile. A month of bed rest made me incredibly eager to get up. Also, my intensive physiotherapy session would begin and I was hoping that would trigger the start of some movement in my legs. I was desperate to get in the gym and give it my all.

The morning arrived and along came the nurse with the revolting looking hoist. Am I really going to have to use that? I was not keen, but the negative thoughts were pushed to the side by the desire to get up out of bed.

It felt so undignified being winched up and helped just to get out of bed. I managed the chair for 30 minutes but it was a struggle and I had to be tipped backwards in the chair several times. This increased my blood pressure and consequently the queasiness lessened. The thirty minutes in the chair made me more exhausted than a whole day's eventing and I needed to rest after it. I did this twice a day, each time for a little longer than the last.

The other challenge I had alongside this was training my bladder. I had a catheter on constant drain right from the day of my fall. I now had to train it to fill again like a normal functioning bladder. It had a tap on, and over the next few days I turned the tap off for a couple of hours and then I would empty my bladder. It just got it used to filling again. The nurse then came to explain to me what the next stage was.

The conversation reduced me to tears again, as much as I tried to be brave. Reality hit me like a tsunami. I had a lifetime ahead of using a catheter. Learning to do this was another task where I felt like I wanted the ground to open up and swallow me whole.

When the time came, the nurse drew the curtains and explained what I had to do. I was learning to use an intermittent catheter so I didn't have to use a leg bag. She got the catheter out and I had to get in a position so she could use a mirror to show me how the catheter is inserted, and how everything must be absolutely sterile. Clean hands, use lubricating gel, dip catheter in and insert into your urethra. Quite a hassle for just a pee, and of course I wouldn't feel when I needed to go so it was just done on time. Every two hours to start with.

The only good side was that it was another 'task' ticked off the list, so I was closer to going home. I kept thinking this when I felt like I had lost all my dignity, it helped me to cope. My focus was 'when can I get out of here?'

I've always been the type of person who has kept in touch with friends, even those I made right from school days. It showed; I certainly had a fantastic bunch of friends. That diary Mum got me was full of friends visiting. Some people in the hospital had no one, I was so lucky. My Mum came almost every day and it wasn't just down the road. She spent ages talking to me. Often I was upset when she came but she always made me feel better. She was the one person whom I could cry in front of and let my emotions out. She comforted me at the lowest of times when no one else would have been able to; she got me through this. Dad and Sue came about 3 to 4 times a week and again, to see them was also my salvation. Both are saints. Sue would always bring me some nice treats. Tim would come along with Sue or Mum if he could, or he'd ring me.

Selena drove five hours each way to see me, and she certainly perked me up. Much to Selena's dismay, both times she visited me I had moved bays and she had heaps of cards to put up. It wasn't all gloom; with having such wonderful parents and so many lovely friends I had never been so sociable. Sometimes we could laugh so much it hurt.

My horses' vet came with one of my school friends, and their partners. They brought me some balloons shaped like elephants to brighten the bay. They blew them up too full but hung them around the place. These were the exploding elephants. A couple burst. The nurse rushed in with a very angry look on her face. "What is going on? I thought somebody had fallen out the bed." I really didn't think that the noise sounded like that, but she was an odd one. She told my unruly visitors to leave. We had a great evening, but the elephants burst throughout the night, one by one.

Jonathan and I had remained friends, and his phone calls became part of each day, and helped draw my mind from the terrifying thoughts about my future. He even visited me a couple of times; we had a Chinese takeaway and shared many jokes.

Lucinda made a few visits. She even managed it when she had been busy training people and had a very long drive to see me. We had long chats, and she left me with a calendar to cross off each day that I had got through. Each day was a day closer to getting home. Her daughter, Lissa, never failed to pick me up if I was low, and we spent time planning a massive walk party for my miraculous recovery, which hadn't happened yet.

Now I was up in the chair for longer and self-catheterizing, I could start going to my physiotherapy sessions. I could still get nauseous at times especially when getting myself down there in the sluggish, heavy wheelchair. Although I had been doing weights in bed to try to stay strong, I felt as weak as a kitten.

To start with the physiotherapy was just trying to get a sitting balance. It was impossible. My bottom was totally numb and my core was floppy, it was hard to sit without clinging on. I felt chuffed to be starting to work on my recovery but mortified at how useless I was.

One session was on the tilt table, we were trying to get my body used to being upright. As I got to 160° I shouted for the sick bowl, it was passed to me just in time. My blood pressure had dropped. I vomited and was green; the physiotherapist helped me back to the ward. I got back into bed and started to feel better. I was disappointed in myself. I had good days, bad days, and horrific days.

Sometimes the self-catheterizing went well, other times I had several pee accidents. The bed could be soaking. I remember clearly the bed had already been changed once but my bladder leaked again later. The nurse glared at me and tutted. I could have smacked her; it was terrible enough without being made to feel like it was my fault. I put my head in my hands and cried. It was like being a baby again; my future looked grim. There were times when I just wished I'd hit the tree a bit harder.

In the new bay to which I had been moved, there was an elderly lady named Marg. She was in her 90s, had dementia and had fallen down the stairs, breaking her neck. She was a lovely old lady, and it was sad to see such a cruel end to her life. Time and time again, during the night, she would scream, "Where am I? Am I dead?" In the daytime I would wheel over and chat to her, try to reassure her. She thought I was her daughter at one point, she was very confused. When she died I was sad, but also relieved to know that she was no longer suffering.

I had spent the last few years focusing on training my horses, and focusing on myself. The morning on which I had been leaving to go to Burghley and we had found swelling in Bob's legs, I'd felt dreadful. Leaving the cross-country course at Burghley felt like the world had crashed down. This journey I was now on, was putting things into perspective. I saw young lads unable to move any of their limbs. In physiotherapy they worked on getting the smallest movement in their head.

There were two ways of looking at things: I was having the worst time I could ever imagine or I was extremely lucky. It was a rollercoaster of feelings that I had. It was also a journey that made me a better person, but of course I didn't know that at the time.

The physiotherapy treatment I was getting was not what I expected. My physiotherapist thought I was brave sitting on the edge of the bed and not being scared of falling. I do not think they understood I was an event rider. How could sitting on the edge of the bed be scary? So what if I did wobble off, it wasn't far to fall.

I got only three sessions per week for 45 minutes. Too frequently I would be asked: "What would you like to do today?" They gave me no inspiration to get on at all. I wanted to do everything I could to give myself the best chance of things improving. "Can I use the bike over there please?" I asked. "There is no point, unless your legs show some sign of movement," came the response. I went on to do more arm movements. I felt very annoyed by their attitude. And this wasn't the first time I had felt negativity in that place.

Right from the start of my journey at the spinal unit, talk of recovering any movement or sensation was called 'false hope' or 'denial'. Why are they so scared of 'some hope'? I was not being unrealistic.

I knew the severity of my injury but surely it was right for me to hope, and to give my recovery my best shot. One of my friends had bought me a bottle of champagne. A nurse walked past and said: "What is that for?" I replied: "I am keeping it for when I can walk." He looked at me and in a disapproving voice said; "What if you don't?" Thankfully I was surrounded by positive thinking friends and family who thought the opposite.

It was obvious they had all been trained to try to get us to accept the injury straight away, and they treated us all the same whether old or young, fit or never done any exercise. I was told this was my new life and I would make new friends now. I now hated people in wheelchairs; a hatred made worse by the people who would wheel over to your bedside with a magazine with a person in a wheelchair on the cover. They would be doing this to tell you 'life goes on in the chair' and what you can still do. This was far too early for me. It made me even more desperate to get out of this place. If they were trying to get me to give up hope and to accept it, I could be the patient to stay the longest in a spinal unit.

It was at two sessions of occupational therapy each week, also known as 'nursery' where they would teach me those basic everyday tasks. It started with learning to sit up in bed from lying, to sit up without the use of the electric hospital bed. Something that was so simple, but now with no core strength, it was a huge effort. I would now have to grip the bed and pull myself up, but I could get a strong spasm which made it even more difficult. I had lessons in dressing, transferring from chair to bed, and worked on a better sitting balance. For the transfers we were given a sliding board, which is just a shiny bit of wood that I could put under my bottom and slide along to get to the bed, car, sofa etc.

A few sessions were spent filing and smoothing my own slide board. Every now and then the occupational therapist would emerge from her office to come out and see me. "Still a little rough here," she would point out as she ran her fingers along the slide board. I couldn't believe it. This young girl with an overly-smiley face was treating me like I had a brain injury. "Keep going, you are getting there." Leaving me feeling patronised she would then disappear off again but I completed my masterpiece. I would soon be able to go home, now I could slide into the car. My next occupational therapy session was filing again, this time a tray for my legs so I didn't burn them. I was told I could stick my favourite picture on it when it was complete. This would be followed by a lesson in the 'dwarf kitchen' they had.

There was a young girl with a broken back. She was only fifteen. She had started to gain movement after a few weeks, and I would go into physiotherapy and see her up on the parallel bars. I was thrilled to see her improvements, and in some ways it spurred me on, but I wondered why it couldn't be me. There was no doubt she was a gutsy girl and her determination helped.

I gave it 100 percent trying to move my legs each day for hours. Recovery depends on how much damage there is to your spinal cord. I thought I had started to be able to flicker a foot, it was exciting - especially to my family. I think I knew though, it was more of a spasm that I could trigger somehow, but it gave me more motivation to carry on just in case this was the start of something more.

I had been bought a laptop by Mum and Dad; it was a lifeline, along with my phone, and an iPod bought for me by my brother.

I spent hours searching for information on recovery and rehabilitation I could do. I found a website called 'Project Walk'. It was a spinal cord injury rehabilitation centre in the USA. They believed you must stimulate your legs to give them any chance of working. This was the opposite of what it was like in hospital where they never worked my legs. In hospital I was also told that because my legs were not moving and because of the poor circulation, my feet would swell and I would need shoes a size bigger now. There was no advice how to reduce the swelling. Did it never occur to them that moving them might help?

I was alarmed by how rapidly my legs were wasting. I had toned legs from riding and now they looked twig-like. The nurse said: "Your legs will waste but it doesn't matter, they're no use to you now." She was a kind nurse and did not mean it to be horrible or negative, it is just what she had been taught and believed. I was a 27 year-old woman. It was important to me to know how I could prevent all the hideous things happening. I didn't want fat feet with spindly legs. They never gave me any advice how to prevent this. This was why I went elsewhere.

The weather that summer suited my mood. It rained and it poured. The floods in Sheffield were about the worst in the country. I had visitors every day but there were two days when Mum couldn't reach me, despite spending five hours in the car. Sheffield was gridlocked. I missed her, but used the days to research things online. Then I heard a familiar voice. I looked round and saw Lucinda in a long mac, absolutely dripping. Only Lucinda would manage this. Somehow she parked up and walked over. I cannot explain what this meant to me. I was seated in my chair clocking up the hours I'd spent in it, and Lucinda was lying on my bed. The afternoon was spent listening to some fascinating stories Lucinda told me.

By now, I had achieved all the things I needed to do before my first day home. I was confident I would be fine for the weekend but the doctors said one day was plenty at this stage. I was so looking forward to seeing the outside world again. Shane picked me up on the Saturday morning. I was so delighted when he walked into my ward to find me. I had been waiting six weeks for this day. I successfully slid into his car. I knew the day would include a combination of emotions but I was mainly just thrilled to be driving away from the hospital.

Seeing roads, fields and trees – yes, even trees – again was a wonderful feeling; it was the feeling I had been craving for. I had been warned that going home could be very upsetting as your last memories there were as an active able-bodied person. Of course I felt some sadness but this was outweighed by the pleasure I got from being back where I belonged.

I wheeled myself to see Roland; he was grazing in the field. Mum helped me get over the grass; it was not easy in the chair. He came over instantly. Roland gave the best cuddle you could wish for. Some people have since asked me if I felt anger towards him. He never asked to be an event horse; it was my decision, as was the risk I took. If Roland knew I was in the chair because I was injured and it was him I was riding, he would be mortified. He was the gentlest horse I had. It was brilliant to see he was fine. I bet Dad felt like shooting him after some of the days he had spent with me in the hospital, but I still loved him.

Tim came over for lunch with Mum, Dad and me. I didn't want a big fuss on my first day back, a quiet lunch was perfect. Just being out of the hospital helped my appetite which wasn't back to normal yet.

Mum and Dad took me back to Sheffield that evening. The day had made me tired. Sitting up for all those hours was demanding; I could get very sore and achy. As soon as I was back in hospital I started planning my next trip home. I had managed fine and decided I would have the whole weekend next time.

By this time I was needing very little help from the nurses. I could do most things myself now. I still used the shower trolley, rather than a chair, so they did assist me getting in and out of the wet room. I was now doing my own transfers on and off the bed. My focus was on proving I could do all this at home. The weekly ward rounds continued, when the doctors came to my bedside to discuss my progress. They would usually stick pins in me to see if I could feel any more. Each week I could see there was no improvement, and I hated to be reminded of it.

I never showed any emotion in front of them and rarely asked a question. I just wanted them to go; I didn't want to ask anything because I knew I would always get an answer I didn't want to hear. The best thing for me was to have a laugh with them about anything, but I limited any talk on spinal injuries.

It was a good job visitors kept pouring in because I didn't have much to do. They had great facilities; a hydro-pool, sports hall, gym, but nothing was used much. I think they struggled financially. For whatever reason, I was offered very little. On a good day I might get one and a half hours of therapy but that was unusual. There were often four days with nothing. I asked to use the gym but was not allowed. I couldn't stand this level of boredom. I had a sports session once in the whole time I was there; I played ping pong and told everyone I won. What I didn't say was my opponents had neck injuries and had little use in their arms. My drive to get on and do my own rehabilitation gave me a goal.

The day I was leaving for my first weekend at home I had a physiotherapy session and went up to my ward to wait for my friend Julie, who was picking me up. I wheeled in to the ward and the nurse said the doctor wanted a word with me. 'Here we go,' I thought, they are going to try to stop me. Julie had arrived at this point. I thought about it and the only thing they could do to make it impossible would be to refuse to give me any catheters, pee bags and gloves. I felt like a naughty school child as I raided the storage cupboard to get all I needed and packed it in my bag.

The doctor turned up to speak to me. "Claire, I hear you think you are going home until Sunday?" He said, looking concerned. "Great news, isn't it? I am so excited" I responded, giving him a big smile. There was an awkward pause before he dropped the bombshell: "No-one goes home for two nights this early after an injury like yours." I looked him in the eye and said: "Well, I am. Julie is here to get me."

I was off like a rocket. I told the nurses to expect me back on Sunday and I would call them if I needed any advice.

This trip home was as exciting as going to a three-day event. My own bed, peace at night, cuddle with my boyfriend, tasty food, fresh air, family and friends. This was going to be paradise. The seven weeks I had experienced made me appreciate the smaller things in life.

It was brilliant except the first night I didn't sleep as well as I had hoped. I had been looking forward to spending the night with Tim, only to find things were not as I expected. I did not feel he was pleased in any way that I was back. One of my main worries was whether my relationship would last now that I was paralysed. If Tim didn't want me then no one else would. After all I was now flat footed, spindly legged, with a flabby tummy, and felt useless. This played on my mind. It took me a while to get to sleep even though it was special being at home and in my own bed. Tim turned over and went to sleep quickly whilst I lay there awake and worrying. My head wouldn't rest for all the thoughts about my future, and already I felt rejected. I eventually nodded off and was in a deep sleep dreaming about my old life again when my alarm clock went off at 1:00 am.

I had to turn every three hours throughout the night to prevent pressure sores. This was an improvement from every two hours which the nurses had been doing. I had been given strict instructions to do this as pressure sores are beastly things. People with spinal cord injuries are prone to them because of the lack of sensation and poor circulation.

People usually turn in their sleep, often unaware. If they become uncomfortable they change their position. I had to move the cushions that were between my knees to stop the knee pressure, and one from behind my back. It was an ordeal to do this turning, and it usually made me wake up completely, especially by the time I had catheterized as well.

The weekend was full on. I did a lot of socializing including a 90th birthday party of a dear friend, Mr. Holmes. It was the loveliest day but it was also incredibly tough. I knew a few people there and everybody was very kind. I had my bravest face on but inside I was in agony.

When Mr. Holmes came into the marquee, everyone stood. I was embarrassed that I couldn't and it felt as though I stood out like a sore thumb. I felt as if everyone was looking at me and feeling sorry for me. The party was very special which is why I went, but I found it to be just too much at this stage. It was such early days. I got through the day and I really had wanted to see Mr. Holmes on such a milestone of a birthday. In the evening there was a hog roast at my parents' holiday log cabins and restaurant, 'Eye Kettleby Lakes'. I was surrounded by some of my closest friends and we had some laughs. Although it left me shattered, I had a better night's sleep.

The following day I had time alone, time to think and to get some rest after the hard day before. Mum and Dad had brought me a bed into their lounge, this was now my bedroom. They really were exceptional at getting things sorted for me. Ramps were installed and my clinic room was converted to a wet room. I was grateful for all of this as it made being at home so much easier. I did see the loss of my chiropractic clinic as closure on my career though. I sat in my clumpy wheelchair and looked at the beautiful fields with the horses in them. Everything had come to a grinding halt. My life was here but everything had changed so much. How was I going to get through this? Could I get through this? What if I couldn't?

On the Monday morning I travelled back to Sheffield with my friend Henry. It wasn't the best job to get, much better to be bringing me home. Henry and I had been close friends since meeting at Hartpury three-day event in 2002. We always had banter and gave each other a hard time. So it could only be Henry who would attempt to help me with my transfer out of the car once we got to Sheffield, and bash my head on the car roof. "Henry, that is one of the few places on my body I can feel. Thanks for that!"

I got back in time for another short 45 minute physiotherapy session, and then it was back to my bay. I did meet a few people whilst in there but there was not really anyone whom I became friends with. There were many elderly patients and young lads, but hardly any females under 50.

By now, I had been in touch with Project Walk in America, and was considering going there for a week to get a home programme. I had also been recommended the name of a neuro-physio close to home so on my list of 'things-to-do' was a call to her.

I really questioned why I was still in the hospital. I had managed fine at home, and I was feeling much better in myself, for which I do owe my thanks to the medical staff. However there was not enough for me to do in this place, at this stage in my rehabilitation.

Mum and Sue visited the next day, plus two friends who had come from Wiltshire. We all went out for a meal in Sheffield.

I did not have any physiotherapy or occupational therapy the next day so I started thinking again. 'What was the point of sitting here in hospital, when I could be at home?' I decided to go home. As we drove back to hospital to pick up what I would need, I was so excited. It was like skiving from school. I rang Tim to tell him the great news but I broke down in tears when he sounded displeased that I was coming home. His response had been that he was supposed to be going for a drink with his mate. I was comforted by Mum, this took a while but I calmed down.

It was a massive slap around my face after being in hospital for two months. I thought he would sound as thrilled as me, but it was quite the reverse. I still managed to enjoy Mum's cooking and my own bed. I returned to Sheffield in time for the weekly meeting, which used to be the Ward round. Now I was mobile we went to a room to meet with the team. We all queued in our chairs like we were going into the teacher's office.

"Next!" was called; it was my turn. I wheeled in not quite sure what to expect. I sat in the centre of the room filled with a team of physiotherapists, occupational therapists, nurses and doctors. It was quite intimidating to say the least and it got worse. "So, how are you getting on Claire?" "Fine thanks," I replied. "How is your bowel management going?" they asked. I couldn't believe I was being asked about my poo in front of twelve people, some I hadn't even met. They sure knew how to make you feel uncomfortable.

I kept my answers brief, I wanted to get out that room as soon as possible. They did say: "We do know you went home," as though I had been naughty. I replied: "Yes, it was good thanks."

"Claire, do you think we know anything?" "A little bit," I said with what must have been a slight smirk. "Well, let me tell you, I have worked with spinal injuries for years, and you need to slow down." On that note I wheeled myself out – slowly.

I made a big decision. I was going to discharge myself from hospital. I could do more rehabilitation at home. Mum was with me on the morning I told the nurses. My family completely understood my decision and they could see how little I was doing at the hospital.

The nurses were shocked. I had not been in the rehabilitation ward for very long and apparently this didn't happen very often. I was sent a person from each area to talk to me: nurses, doctors, physiotherapists and an occupational therapist. They all had to give their reason why I should stay. I did not feel anyone had given me a valid reason.

The physio was very sharp with me and repeated what they told me previously: "If your legs show any sign of movement we will work them but there is nothing there." This was exactly the attitude I didn't like, so it made me feel like I was making the right decision. In Occupational Therapy, no longer had I got to stick my favourite picture on to my extremely well filed tray, nor had I to have the 'boiling a kettle' lesson in the dwarf kitchen.

The consultant was lovely. He explained clearly the reason they were concerned. He thought physically I would be fine but mentally I was a long way from accepting it. He had hardly seen me upset, I had asked little and it concerned him. I was on a mission to get out throughout my rehab and this gave me a goal. I didn't ask much because I didn't want to hear their pessimistic answers. He was also concerned that I would not see people in wheelchairs and would feel alone. All the more reason to leave, I liked that idea. Being surrounded by spinal injuries all the time could never let me forget the injury for a second.

He also explained how a spinal injury is similar to the feelings of losing a loved one. I had to grieve for the loss, and I had all that to come. This made sense, but I needed to grieve at home, not in a hospital.

I was certain I was doing the right thing, and confirmed to the nursing staff I was going to leave. As I packed my things, one nurse had the nerve to say to my mum: "What kind of a mother are you?"

I was old enough to make my own mind up. I was disgusted someone could say that to Mum, who had been a super-Mum the whole time, day in, day out.

They then asked how I would get out of the car into my house. As I knew they were obsessed by false hope I replied: "I'll just have to walk won't I?" They were not amused.

I was then told that I couldn't borrow their wheelchair to get out to the car park at the hospital. It looked like I was going to have to be dragged there. Reluctantly, in the end, they relented and let us. I timed it brilliantly, as I got to the car I had a little accident and Mum returned the chair cushion covered in pee. I was free!

3

I was feeling very relieved to know that part of my journey was complete. The hospital days were over in a relatively short time although it certainly didn't seem like that whilst I was there. I also knew I had some of the toughest days ahead; my battle to come to terms with my new life had only just started. My sole focus over the past few weeks had been to get out of hospital. Now I needed to find new goals, which wasn't going to be simple.

Mum and Dad had been so supportive about my overwhelming desire to be back home and had made the house easy for me to live in. My neighbours had wanted to get me a gift so they all contributed to making my wet room look special. It was full of gifts; body lotions, shampoo, towels, soap and plants. It was such a lovely surprise for me to come home to. We had the local occupational therapy lady visit before I discharged myself from hospital and there was now a shower chair in there too.

We pulled up at home; Mum nipped in to the wet room to get the shower chair to help me get out of the car into the house. There was always a solution to every problem. Mum rang the Red Cross, and the next day I had the loan of a wheelchair until I got my own which was going to be fairly soon.

I didn't want too much time alone to think as it would be easy to slip into depression so I tried to make sure I saw friends each day as well as allow some essential rest time. It was easy to forget that only nine weeks ago I was in the I.T.U. seriously ill. It was inevitable I would get tired because my body was still healing.

I would frequently be having lunch out, and it wasn't unusual for me to not want to, but I made myself do it. I was often asked by my friends: "Are there any improvements?" They were desperate to hear I had some encouraging signs but I had to constantly say no. Hearing myself say that was agony, every little cell in me wanted to reply with a yes. It was essential I went out even though it was such a struggle. My lovely friends would distract me and we would share laughs like old times. Some of my close friends would help me with my exercises during their visit. I found out who my true friends were, the majority were exceptional, and no one dropped me because of my life changing accident.

The day came for me to get my own wheelchair ordered. The NHS either gave you a basic wheelchair or a voucher for £500 to go towards a better one. To me a wheelchair was just a means of getting around, and I didn't want to spend my money on one so I decided to go with what the NHS offered. The lady showed me the choices. "Do you like this one?" she said. I looked at her, "Not really," I replied. She showed me a few more; same reply. In the end the lady smiled and said: "Do you hate this one a little less than that one?" That is how I chose my chair.

I hated them all with a vengeance. I felt angry that I needed one. I was now classed as a disabled person. My life was ruined forever. At least that is what I thought at the time.

Project Walk and I had been exchanging emails. We made the decision to go there for a week. With no hesitation we got our flights and accommodation booked. I was going to have three hours each day in the gym and be given a programme to follow at home. I was apprehensive about the long flight to L.A. but this kind of positivity was exactly what I needed and what I had been searching for.

I had spoken to the doctor about some NHS physiotherapy, as well as getting in touch with the private neuro-physiotherapist who had been recommended. The doctor arranged for an NHS physiotherapist, named Suzi, to come once a week. This worked well because the two physiotherapists actually knew each other. Both Suzi and Kate came out to assess me, before I went to Project Walk. They were both fantastic. It was exciting to think I now had two physios to work with who both had similar views to me. They were keen to help me, and they started by giving me some kneeling exercises to do, before I set off to Project Walk.

Mum, Dad, Tim and I set off to Project Walk near San Diego. This was far from a holiday. The flight from Gatwick to L.A. was stressful. Trying to use the small loo was one of the hardest things I had ever tried to do. I could have easily had a breakdown in there and never come out. I was both frustrated and angry that having a pee could be so traumatic. I wore special stockings, supposedly to help stop my legs from swelling, but of course the combination of flying and being paralysed meant they soon started to swell and they became massive. I hated seeing my legs look like tree trunks, and it made transferring more difficult as they weighed a ton. I was still taking Warfarin to thin the blood to prevent blood clots.

After a very long day we arrived at the bungalow we had booked for the week. It was a beautiful place and we were near the coast. The weather was perfect. Our bungalow was close to the rehabilitation centre, making it easy to travel in each day, in the car we'd hired. I had a couple of days to recover from the long flight; I managed to have a good rest before I started the intensive week of rehabilitation.

I had studied videos and photos of Project Walk whilst I was stuck in hospital so had a good idea what to expect. There was a massive gym with stacks of specialized equipment for spinal injured patients. The trainers were all quite young with ample amounts of energy. My trainer for the week came and introduced herself. She was fairly small but very fit looking and strong. Her name was Lee and I liked her, which was a relief as I had a fair few hours working closely with her.

The first thing I had to do was get on the floor and roll. They videoed me so I had the film to take home to watch and to continue the work. I felt like a beached whale trying to roll, and a bit stupid to be honest. I hated being filmed but it was going to be for my own benefit, so I had to put up with it.

At the time I had my accident there were no centres like Project Walk in the U.K that ran rehabilitation programmes for spinal injured people, as far as we could see. Their theory all made sense. If you placed an able-bodied person in a reduced gravity environment, told them they couldn't move for a year, heavily medicated them and gave them no hope, that able-bodied person would have the same symptoms as a paralysed person.

When I read all their information I knew I had to give my recovery all my effort, and even if I didn't make any notable improvements I would be fit and healthy. This surely would help prevent some of the common complications associated with having a spinal injury, such as reduced bone density, muscle atrophy, poor circulation, pressure sores, etc. I knew it was the right road for me to go down.

The week at Project Walk included floor work and using some of the equipment they had in the gym. They also got me up on my feet with the help of therapists and a rail to hold on to. I smiled a genuine smile because I felt tall again; where I should be, on my very own two feet.

It was so refreshing to be in a room of people who were all really positive and working hard to give their injuries the best chance to improve. The team at Project Walk made it clear that the clients who made the best recovery were the ones who also got on with their lives, not only to do rehabilitation but to do other things as well.

When we were not at Project Walk, we filled the rest of our time over there exploring the area but I knew I was there for one reason and for one reason only. I felt too low to enjoy much. We did go to the coast and we had a meal there. It was stunning but all I could see whilst looking out at the golden sand and blue sea were people running, supreme athletes with slim and gorgeous bodies, who made running look so easy. I had never quite looked like them but I had been slim, very fit and able to run effortlessly. This was painful to the extreme. Why did this have to happen to me?

I'd spent hours and hours struggling to try to get my legs to show some sign of life. I felt trapped inside a body that had let me down. I wanted to run free from this, I have never wished for anything as much as I did for this. Turning back the time was not an option, no one could change my situation. The only thing I could do was exactly what I was doing – to keep trying and never to give up; you never know what the future has in store.

I picked myself up and continued my therapy. I left Project Walk with a booklet of exercises to share with Suzi and Kate. I had gained so much useful knowledge and so many new and good ideas for exercises I could work on.

Once I got home, it took time to recover from the trip. After all, I was still supposed to be in hospital. It was quite an ordeal but we soon got into a routine, with the help of my physiotherapists, we worked on the home programme. We hoped to return to the States, to spend a month out there the following January, and Kate would possibly come for a week too.

In some ways the weeks that followed were the hardest ones of my life. I always did my exercises and physio sessions no matter how low I felt, but there were times of genuine despair.

My body shape had changed dramatically and despite being careful not to eat too much or to put on weight, I still couldn't fit in my clothes. Not only could I not fit in them but the style would no longer suit me. I could not wear clingy tops, I needed high waisted trousers otherwise I would show a builder's bum each time I transferred from one thing to another. I couldn't wear tight trousers without a battle to get in and out of them, and high heels were a definite no.

Maybe a shopping spree would cheer me up and give me a choice of outfits in my wardrobe to rebuild my confidence. I was naturally drawn to the same clothes as before my accident but I soon realised how unsuitable they were. I started selecting the things that I thought I might look OK in but the choice was limited. The cubicles were cruel; there were mirrors surrounding me and very little space. I just was not allowed to escape from seeing the unpleasant and disgusting sight that was me. I had to get out of the shop quickly, before I went crazy. It was another disaster and failed attempt to find some new clothes.

With a spinal injury it is the shock of so many changes all of a sudden; there is no time to adapt. I felt as if I was going from one bad experience to another. With catheterizing, for example, you are prone to urine infections and the trouble was I didn't always know when I had mild infections. If I had stayed in hospital longer I might have been more aware of this. The infection causes the bladder to keep emptying so I had days when I would pee myself, struggle in the shower, get dressed, only for it to happen again and again. It was days like this when I lost the will to live; what sort of life was I living?

I would shut myself away and cry until I had no more tears left. I didn't want to see anyone or do a thing, not even talk on the phone. Then somehow I would find a way of pulling myself out of this self-pitying, depressive state. I don't know exactly what would make me bounce back, but deep inside me there was the will to fight and not to let my loved ones down.

I knew that I was going to have to try riding again so four months after my accident Tim lent me a quiet skewbald horse to ride called Queenie. She was a gentle girl and suitable for me to try to ride again, but she couldn't have been more different from my event horses. My first day back in the saddle was in the presence of Selena, Tim and Mum. It was quite an achievement to be back on this early, in lots of ways I was quite proud. Selena snapped away taking photos and we joked about Queenie being my next Burghley horse. It was excellent therapy for core strengthening and improving my balance. I was riding her for half an hour. It gave me some fresh air and exercise but it was far from exciting. My body was broken but my mind remained the same and walking a quiet horse down the road was hardly ever a thrill before my accident.

One of my horses was competing at a local horse trial so we decided to take Queenie to the event for me to

55

ride around. The doctors would have been horrified if they could see what I was up to. I spent most of the day on her. It did feel better than being in the wheelchair because I could chat to friends on an eye-to-eye level instead of looking up, and on a horse you couldn't tell that I was paralysed. When I got close to the cross-country course Queenie started to get excited. She began to jog and bounce around and whilst it scared me to death, it also gave me the adrenaline rush I so badly needed.

We loaded Queenie back in the lorry and headed over to the score boards. Wheelchairs do not move at all well on grass, and in stony gateways they are even worse. Sue was helping me but we were all novices with wheelchairs. She tripped on a stone and kept hold of me. We ended up with me, still in the wheelchair, lying on top of Sue. I could have died with embarrassment, and hoped nobody had seen us. "Get me up," I said, "quick!" We brushed ourselves down, kind of chuckled, and carried on.

I had won this event last year on highly rated Bart, but this year was somewhat different. There were no rosettes for managing to shout: "Get me off" when Queenie started to get lit up, or for when I had squashed Sue. Laugh or cry? Both sometimes.

Mum knew a lady who had had a horse riding accident many years ago. She had been in touch and kindly offered for me to try out her car with the hand controls. I went over to see her and tested them out. It wasn't too difficult and I felt confident enough to order a car through the Motability scheme. I ordered the same hand controls as she had in her car.

It was November when I got my own new car. Mum drove it back from the garage so I could get used to it on quieter roads. It still had the foot controls in but with a lever attached so that I could control them using a push and pull motion. To begin with I got the movements confused and pushed to accelerate which brought me to a grinding halt. When this occurred on a roundabout with Henry in the car on one of our weekly trips out people beeped at me and glared. We laughed, but I noticed that Henry was now looking a bit tense. Whilst I was in the car I felt free from my spinal injury. I was driving like everyone else; I had just gained some independence back and normality.

I was trying my best to stay positive but it was impossible. My relationship was far from good, it was falling to pieces and so was I. It was a Saturday evening, I was in, alone, with Tim, but there was little conversation. I picked up one of the magazines that I had been given whilst in hospital; it was full of information on spinal injuries. I was terrified by what I read. It was full of complications and information on how to manage different areas of your life. The section on relationships said that it was common for them to break down; this catastrophic injury was bound to affect everyone around me, some partners would cope and others would not. I felt certain that Tim didn't want me anymore and it was horrible living like that, but for now I decided I would carry on. I wasn't ready for another change in my life, not just yet.

Adapting to life with a spinal cord injury was beyond challenging. Having lost all sensation from the chest down was strange. I would pinch my leg to see if I could feel anything in desperate hope of some improvements but I couldn't feel a thing to the touch. Yet the nerve pain was often uncomfortable; tingling, burning, pins and needles constantly reminded me that I was paralysed. I was lying in bed and I was convinced that my legs were in a certain position. I frightened myself to death when I felt a leg on the other side of my bed. Who the hell had got into bed with me? Of course, it was my own leg, but as I put my hand on it and there were no messages telling me it was my leg I automatically thought it was someone else's. The importance of feeling pain is only too well highlighted by an incident one summer evening when we had a BBQ in the garden. . I was sitting close to it but totally unaware I was sizzling my leg. Thankfully it was noticed before there was any serious damage, but I had quite a nasty burn that scarred me. It is now a reminder of the first year; the toughness of coming to terms with everything and learning about my broken body.

Hazel and Sue, Bob's groom, had been to visit me a couple of times; even on one of my better days, it left me feeling upset. It felt wrong not to mention Bob but I was so hurt by the way they had replaced me whilst I was still in intensive care. I had spoken to Jeanette once now, because Lucinda kindly had a word with her and suggested she gave me a call. I asked her to let me know how he got on at his events but I heard no more. She never asked me anything about the horse. I felt really cut off.

Burghley Horse Trials were here again, and Bob was entered as I had expected at the beginning of the season. The heart-breaking thing is I was watching from the competitors' tent in a wheelchair. After much deliberation as to whether I should go or not, I decided to go. Either way it was going to be extreme misery and torment. I went for three of the four days. With it being a local event I bumped into so many people I knew. I was asked the same questions time and time again, and I tried to put the brave smiley face on. Inside I was bleeding. There were times we would see people I didn't want to see, Sue or Mum would suddenly hear me say: "Turn left, turn left." I needed help on the grass again, but we were careful that we didn't fall over this time. By the end of the three days I tried not being so brave, and when I was asked how I was feeling I just replied: "Crap, thanks." It did mean I got asked fewer questions.

As soon as I got there Tim disappeared to walk the cross country course, clarifying what I already knew about our relationship. I watched Bob go cross-country from the competitors' tent. Last year I was living my dream, now I was living a total nightmare. To see a different rider on him felt really surreal, Bob was my ride. I had so many photos and videos of him at home from a young horse up to this top level. Lucinda sat on one side of me and Mum the other. Bob looked good as I expected but a stop in the main arena caused me to smile a little through my streaming tears. Jeanette was interviewed like all the other riders after completing. I admit, I was upset when she didn't mention my 5 years of training him into the 4-star horse he was. There did not seem any concern about my pain, or if there was she certainly didn't show it. On our way out we passed Hazel and Sue. I wound the window down and said: "Well done!" "Thank you. We are on such a high!" came the response. There was not a mention that they wished I was still riding, nothing. I had always thought we were a great team, and I still think we were but I realised they were not my true friends. That hurt. I could have gone into a downward spiral after this but one friend put a stop to that. The few horrific days at Burghley were followed by a couple of days with non-stop laughs and planning.

Lissa came to stay. Most of the time was spent pondering over which event riders we thought would get their kit off for a naked calendar. A fellow event rider,

Rachel Robinson, whom I'd met once on a Lucinda training day, and had then parked next to her on the day of my accident, had sent me emails during my hospital days. She was extremely thoughtful and kind natured and she had decided that some fundraising should be done to help me to get the equipment I needed, and to go back to Project Walk. It was she who came up with the idea of the semi-naked event riders' calendar. Lissa and I had great fun asking the riders, planning the scenes and approaching sponsors. It was the perfect distraction.

We had to crack on with it soon as we were already in September. This took all of the next month, and it did heaps for me mentally. I was touched by how generous people were. We had two photo shoots, one in Leicestershire and one in Wiltshire. Not only did the riders give up their time but the photographers did too. A printing company called SR Communications even offered their support; it was a real success and the ideal horsey Christmas present.

Selena wanted to help to fundraise too and she organized a lecture demonstration at Merrist Wood in Surrey with show jumper Tim Stockdale. My friends and even strangers were getting together and raising money to enable me to push on with my fight to walk again one day. Another kind friend, Hannah set up a website and the 'Get Claire Walking Campaign' began.

I was given the best chance to keep up my rehab but most importantly this kept my spirits up, I owed it to all these people to keep going.

A couple of years before my accident I remembered hearing of a local rugby player who was left paralysed from the neck down, his name is Matt Hampson. Matt's injury was about as severe as you can get, he relied on a ventilator to breathe. On the days I didn't leave my room I usually switched on the laptop and read about things that might inspire me. I started looking at articles about Matt and I was blown away by his immense courage and his 'live-life-to-the-full' attitude. He was only 20 when he had his rugby accident, yet it seemed he had a remarkably mature attitude. I got in touch with Matt, a mutual friend gave me his number and we arranged to meet up.

Matt has had a big influence on my life and he will never know how much he helped me. I had always looked up to the top event riders, as that is what I wanted to do, but I now admired this young man for the guts he had shown so as to cope with the cards he was dealt. By his example, he showed me that no matter how bad the injury, life is what you make it. Always, he came across as being very confident and happy in himself. I soon didn't see his chair or his ventilator, I just saw a guy with a wicked sense of humour whom it was great to be around.

I had two choices with my life: I could dwell on all the negative aspects and stay miserable. The alternative, which was much more appealing, was to get out there and make the most of things. I learned a lot that day, and I went home thinking about the future in a far more positive light.

I spent all of January 2008 at Project Walk. Mum and I were there for four weeks and joined by Dad, Sue, Gill and Kate, all for a week each. I spent two hours each week day in the gym with weekends off. I had different trainers to work with, some excellent and some quite disappointing. I didn't know who I had until I arrived each morning. I learned to use a gait trainer where I was in a harness standing upright and the machine moved my legs in a similar pattern to walking. This was in an attempt to stimulate the nervous system and any muscle memory. Kate was an exceptional neuro-physiotherapist. Like all talented and knowledgeable people, she always wanted to learn more, which is why she spent a week with us. She watched what they did at Project Walk, knowing that we could take away the aspects we thought were working well for me.

We spent most spare days sunbathing or shopping, as the clothes were so cheap compared to the U.K. I had managed to find quite a few things I actually liked for a change, in Ralph Lauren. I was sitting in the queue waiting to purchase a couple of items when I heard a 'trickle' noise. It was a shiny marble tiled floor, now with a puddle of pee in the middle. "Oh my god, Mum, I have pissed," I said. "What shall I do?" We decided to put the clothes to one side and leave the shop. We went back and laughed about it, this injury was certainly character building.

We also tried some trips out including Sea World, but I only made it to the car park because when I saw how many people were there, I couldn't face it. We did make it to the zoo but it wasn't really what I liked so it didn't make me feel great.

I hated long days in the chair, I much preferred being in the gym to doing the tourist thing. My thoughts that Tim didn't want me haunted me whilst I was over there. He appeared to have no interest in how I was getting on. He rang once or twice a week but even on the phone he had no spark in his voice. I knew it was coming to an end. I felt so rejected. I got in an emotional state on a few occasions where I was so upset I cried myself to sleep. Maybe I should just put up with the relationship as it was, it would be better than being on my own – or would it?

When I returned home, Tim came over that evening. I thought he would at least pretend to be pleased to see me but it was clear to see that his priority was what he was going to have for dinner, what I had brought back for him from America, and then how had I got on, in that order.

I didn't know what to do, or where to turn. I knew I wasn't coping and, in some ways, Tim was not to blame. I had only to see the mirrors in the changing cubicles to understand why he didn't want me. It made me angry but I knew that I was doing all I could to improve, and to stay fit.

This included standing in a wooden frame for an hour a day. I had straps behind my pelvis and in front of my knees to keep me upright. It was a bright sunny day when Mum put the frame outside so I could get some fresh air. I could get in and out of it myself, but, that day, as I went to sit down my chair moved and I fell to the floor. I was feeling even more fragile than usual at the time, and this almost finished me off. I was alone and I felt absolutely useless. I hated my legs more than ever. Using my hands and arms, I dragged myself up the ramp into the house. The ramp was rough; I could see it taking the skin off and my legs bleeding. They deserved it. I wanted to hurt them. I hated them. I hated myself.

When I was like this, my family struggled. They hated seeing me like this, I knew they wanted to help, but there was nothing they could do. They would suggest all sorts of different things I could try to do, but when you are in this frame of mind nothing appeals. All I could think about was what I used to do and the things I had lost. I didn't seem to want to try much else yet. It could only happen when I was ready.

Since being a child I'd always been a real outdoors person, so being cooped up in my room for so many hours at a time was totally out of character. "Get outside, Claire, fresh air will make you feel better," Mum would say trying her best to help. "What – park on the ramp like a disabled person? Great, bloody great!" would be the response.

When I was in a negative, self-pitying mood I could not think of anything I would ever want to do as much as I'd wanted to do eventing.

It was my birthday the next day and Tim was supposed to be taking me out for dinner, but when I spoke to him I got the feeling he couldn't be bothered to anymore. He was letting me down on my birthday. This was the final straw. When I told him I had had enough, I could hear the delight in his voice. He had not had the guts to do it himself. I think he had been as distant as he could so as to make me finish it, and I did.

I had felt at my loneliest when I was with Tim. I didn't want to be with someone because they felt sorry for me. I didn't want pity. I started to feel some of my strength return. I was single again and I was relieved. This turned out to be a huge leap forward in my recovery. I could start to move forward now I no longer had a failed relationship dragging me down. It had been doing severe damage to my confidence and to my self-esteem. Perhaps my real recovery could start now.

4

Every day I stood for an hour in my standing frame, with my laptop in front of me and the TV switched on as background noise. It got really boring doing this day after day but it had just become part of my daily routine. On this particular day, I started to flick the channels on the controller and Channel 5 News grabbed my attention. There he was, a young man with a spinal injury walking with a frame. Each step looked as though it was an arduous effort but he was up on his feet.

I was so impressed by what I saw I immediately started searching to find out more. I typed in his name on Google and found his website. This standing session had passed all too quickly. I was intrigued to find out more about how this man had managed to take these steps. I found his email address on his website, and contacted him. His name was Guy. He was keen to share all of his experiences, and we had a long phone call.

Very bizarrely he was injured whilst he was sending a text message and not concentrating on where he was going. He walked straight in front of a lorry, leaving him paralysed from the waist down. He was also diagnosed with a complete injury. A complete injury means that there is no function below the level of injury; no sensation and no voluntary movement.

Guy's experience of rehabilitation in hospital sounded similar to mine, and it had driven him to search for other options. It was a clinic in Central London that had helped him to take steps again, and over time he had recovered significant movement in his legs. He suggested I tried contacting them myself. I didn't ponder and quickly booked my first appointment.

Hratch was certainly different, a bit of a maverick. He was short and fairly stocky with a caricature face and huge

Hratch was certainly different, a bit of a maverick. He was short and fairly stocky with a caricature face and huge droopy moustache. He was a combination of warm and soft, yet tough and aggressive. Hratch believed that the mind had much to do with recovery. He told me that I would need total focus to help me to get back on my feet and total commitment.

I was not daunted by this; after all I had spent years in a sport which demanded commitment and dedication. To see Guy was evidence this had worked. He'd not had even a twitch of movement in his legs for months, so to actually see what he had achieved was awe-inspiring.

Hratch spent time getting me to send signals to my legs, whilst my legs were stimulated by electrical impulses. I was trying to connect pathways from my brain to my legs. He would get me to cycle a special bike, making certain that I was trying my best to push the pedals. Of course I couldn't do it yet but it was all about trying with 100 percent belief and effort.

I had some ankle splints made to measure, and I was soon up on a frame with a safety harness like Guy. I had assistance but we could see progress in the making. Hratch was undoubtedly a one off. I would be shouted at frequently and he would drive me to put maximum exertion into everything I did.

"Move your legs," he would say. Nothing happened. "Are you trying? Come on you lazy cow. Move your f****** legs!" He would shout, sometimes extremely loudly, but I saw it as encouragement. When he got really angry I would just look at him and say: "Shout louder Hratch, get angry," followed by: "Grrr, Hratch, you look so sexy when you get cross." He would fight the grin but not succeed and soon we'd both be laughing: result!

Going to this Clinic was certainly the best thing for me at the time. I needed Hratch in my life. His personality wouldn't have suited everyone but we got on well, and usually gave each other a hard time in a joking manner. I always finished the sessions exhausted, and he gave me the enthusiasm and belief to keep working hard. It was without doubt the right thing for me. I never wanted to regret not having tried hard enough. I needed to do this but I also had to have a life beyond rehab.

Hratch wasn't cheap and every week it was a five hour-long drive. He wanted me to devote the next few years solely to working on my recovery. I soon discovered that I just could not do this. Hratch told me I needed to do hours of this every day, and I was very willing to do that. What I couldn't accept, and thought was wrong, was that he didn't want me to do anything else. He saw it as a distraction but I saw it differently, as having some balance in my life. I have always been the type of person to make my own decisions. I am not a follower. I refused to be brainwashed into this way of working.

I understood the doctor's point of view when they wanted me to just get on with my life in a chair, as there was still so much to be achieved as a paralysed person. Hratch was the opposite, he thought I should give up everything for the rehab and then I would start to see improvements. Guy had done this.

Project Walk were right when they advised me that a balance is what I needed. As I started to do more of the things I enjoyed, the activities which gave me pleasure and helped me to keep things in balance, Hratch didn't like it. I decided I had to leave. It was my life and it was essential I chose the route that I felt suited me best. Life is short; somehow I needed to find happiness.

I knew very little about spinal injuries at the time I had my accident, and all these routes to recovery had to be discovered and then explored. I know that I was very fortunate to be able to; it was thanks to my friends and the eventing community who raised the funds. Leading event riders William Fox-Pitt and Tina Cook did a lecture demo, again organized by Selena, and friends Lucinda and Lottie both did teaching days for me. As well as many other friends raising funds, it was made possible for me to explore all the possible avenues that could help my recovery. I never regretted any of the things I tried. They all helped. I learnt valuable things from them all and I then took from each one the aspects I most liked to then find my own way forward.

A year had passed since my accident and my physio, Suzi, had to leave as I was not allowed any more physiotherapy on the NHS; I had been very lucky to have her for a year. I missed her, she had become a friend. I still had Kate who was my rock. Kate couldn't be more different from Hratch. Sometimes she is perhaps a bit too soft but she is a top class physiotherapist and a sensitive character, and I knew that I would be able to work with Kate for a very long time.

My Dad's friend, Ivor, who is a keen pilot emailed me and suggested I had flying lessons. He knew I needed to find an interest and he very kindly gave me some money so that I could give it a try. I went to a nearby airfield for my first lesson with the British Disabled Flying Association, where they had a specially adapted plane. There was quite a lot of hanging around before I even got into the plane. I felt privileged to have the opportunity to get to fly the plane but sadly, when I did, it didn't give me the excitement, the adrenaline rush, I had hoped for.

We flew over Chatsworth House where one of the important International One Day Event was imminent. I could see that they had started to set up the event. As I looked down from the sky to see this, I couldn't help feeling sad. Immediately I compared flying to eventing and I realised that I didn't find flying even a fraction as exhilarating. I thought that over time I might start to get the buzz from it that I so desperately wanted. I continued to have lessons but there was often at least a month's gap between flights. It seemed it was impossible to ever string a few close together because they had only the one adapted plane and then when I did have a flight booked in, all it took was for the weather not to be ideal and it was cancelled. Although I felt disappointed in myself, as I hate quitting, I decided to tell Ivor that flying was sadly not for me.

The Para-Dressage Performance Director came to see me with a DVD about the sport. People were so very thoughtful to try to help me to find an interest again. The 2012 Paralympics in London were only four years away, and this could give me an ambitious goal to aim for. I had already been considering para-dressage, especially as I knew it was going to be different from riding Queenie. I decided to give it a go and I started by riding a mechanical horse at a local Riding for the Disabled Centre, in an attempt to build up my core strength and to improve my balance.

I was offered a ride on Ivor's daughter's horse, Spark. Although he was not like my event horses, he was a smart horse who'd had considerable success show-jumping and showing. I was really proud to be seen on him, and I often laughed that my spinal injury had improved my dressage. Spark was so well trained. We looked pretty good, better than I'd ever looked on Bob or Roland. This was going to be what I was going to do throughout the summer. I hoped that I would regain some passion for a sport, something for me to get really stuck into and maybe to have dreams again; perhaps London 2012.

Rather to my surprise I found being single so much better than being with someone who was making me feel rubbish about myself. However, I also knew that I was going to turn thirty in a couple of years, and the prospect of being single and in a wheelchair caused me to start wondering and to worry about my future, and it did upset me.

It was the 6th May 2008, exactly a year on from the day that turned my life into a shattered mess. I decided I needed to have some fun, to take my mind off it. Helen, whom I actually met whilst I was in Australia, was also an eventing friend. We decided to meet in Birmingham for lunch and a photo-shoot. The idea of some pampering and a makeover appealed to me. I hoped that, maybe, they would work a miracle and I'd look half decent in the photos to boost my very low confidence. I set off in the morning, and Helen left her home in Wiltshire to meet me before lunch. I wasn't feeling upset and I wasn't thinking about my accident, I was just looking forward to a good day out, a treat.

At what seemed to be the busiest traffic light junction in Birmingham my car decided to pack in. I had put it into park whilst I waited for the lights to change, and when I tried to put it into drive to pull away the automatic gear box was buggered. I couldn't have felt more stranded. I was stuck, I was useless and I was unable to get out of the car on this hectic road even if I had wanted to; my wheelchair was in the back. People were horrible; beeping their horn and shouting at me, as if I had just parked there for the fun of it.

As with most traumas in my life, Mum got a phone call. I was sobbing hysterically. Mum did her best to calm me down. I was probably emotionally on edge that day and this was just too much for me to deal with. I screamed out of the window at the angry drivers, "I can't f******g walk!" I had crumbled.

As soon as Helen arrived I started to feel better. A very kind gentleman walking by helped by pushing my car to the side. I rang the breakdown rescue. They would be coming out to mend it, but it would not be for at least an hour. Our appointment was looming, but my panic had thankfully subsided. We left my car keys at the pub on the corner of a nearby road, and the mechanic picked them up from there.

I grabbed my slide-board, we got in a taxi to get to the studio with a minute to spare. Although I tried to rush, I had to accept the reality that my life now was slow. I had always liked to be quick and punctual, so this was rather annoying to say the least.

It was a good job they plastered make-up on me for these photos to help disguise the sadness in my eyes. We ended up having a really enjoyable afternoon even though it had been somewhat overshadowed by the stress. I arrived home safely and was delighted to be tucked up in bed. I managed to joke that next year on 6th May I was going to stay in bed all day.

It was shortly after this when I had one of those bad spells; it was like having a dark cloud all around me. Everything seemed to be black, and there was no way of seeing the light no matter how hard I tried. I wanted to shut myself off from the world. For a fleeting moment I even thought that maybe an overdose of the paracetamol, lying near me, would release me from this nightmare.

Lissa was coming to stay for a few days; she was nearby staying with another friend. I didn't want to see anyone. Not even Lissa who had the unbelievable ability to lift my mood. When I felt this bad I would turn my phone off and not want to see anyone except Shane, who I could usually see even when at my very worst. I sent Lissa a text saying: "Please don't come, I don't feel well." She didn't get it until she was sitting with me trying to console me. "Oh I've just got your text," she said awkwardly. By then, it was too late. She had to see me in a bad way. For someone nine years my junior, she had so much empathy. I don't know how she did it, but gradually the cloud started to blow away. Rational thoughts must have taken over because I remembered all the true friendship, kindness and generosity that had selflessly been bestowed on me. This was a turning point for me; things were going to slowly start to improve.

Matt Hampson had invited me to a fundraising fashion show in aid of prostate cancer. I had got four tickets for Lissa, Lucy, Anna and myself, a girls' night out. It had looked as if I was not going to be able to go but because Lissa had started to make me feel better I was now feeling up for it.

It was in Leicester and it featured some of the Leicester Tigers rugby players. There was not a better remedy than this to lift my mood. The players paced up and down the catwalk, even underwear was modeled by these fit rugby men. A few glasses of champagne and I started to feel the beneficial effect. I began to feel like the old Claire again. Wonderful, I was having a genuinely brilliant evening.

We went on to a bar after this. It had several steps and was unsuitable for people in wheelchairs - unless the Leicester Tigers rugby team were at hand, that was. There was no hesitation. I was soon carried up the stairs, and my friends were clearly jealous. We got chatting to some lads in there, they seemed a decent bunch. A few more drinks were enjoyed, and I couldn't believe it when I even got a snog. Yes, I pulled! How did that happen, I was in a wheelchair, I was not expecting that at all. He wasn't particularly my type of guy but this night was doing me a shed load of good.

The next thing I knew was that these lads were pushing me like the clappers to the nightclub where we were noisy and had loads of unquestionable fun. We all confirmed that I would walk again, it was just a matter of time, but for now being whizzed around by these lads was entertaining.

I sat in a normal chair in the nightclub, so Lissa saw an opportunity to jump into my wheelchair. "I'm going to do an experiment for you," she said as she zoomed off. Half an hour later she returned. "Bloody hell, I tell you what, you are not going to have a problem getting free drinks in this."

It is hard to believe that one daft drunken night out gave me so much confidence. It was clear to see people treated me just the same as long as I was myself, and that night I was.

It had been a mistake getting the NHS chair, I always needed a lightweight one for independence. I'd had my new chair a while now and I could get this new one in and out the car myself. It took me a while to adapt and I had several falls until I learnt the new balance. I kept the NHS chair as my spare. Typically, when Lissa and I went out into my local town, Melton Mowbray, we took both chairs for a laugh, one for me and one for her. Very naughty I know, but it was highly amusing watching people's reactions when Lissa would suddenly get out of her chair and get something off the top shelf in the supermarket, or when we had pushed ourselves over to the car and she sprang out and loaded the wheelchairs into the car. People were giving us strange looks and yes, we loved it.

A couple of days with Lissa had given me a short break from the repetitive, mundane rehab I did. Now, I was back strapped in the standing frame with my laptop open and finding interesting stuff to read to help pass the time, being nosey about other people's lives.

Lissa must have clicked on an advert for 'Countryside Love' when she'd borrowed my laptop to go on Facebook. Out of curiosity I had a look at the dating website. With time to kill, I filled out my profile, attached a few photos and wrote a short paragraph about myself. I was upfront about my spinal injury but made it clear I was determined to walk one day and that I was an active person. The photos included one each of my eventing, flying, skydiving, a night out and one in my chair - but you could hardly see the chair. Did I expect a message? Absolutely not!

To my surprise, I started to get one or two but there was nothing worth getting excited about or paying the twenty pounds subscription fee to read them. I could see their profile without paying, and they were either too young or too old or just didn't interest me for whatever reason. That was until, after three days on the site, I got a message from Dan and his profile looked all right. After deliberating over whether I should subscribe or not, with friends' persuasion, I did.

We were messaging each other for a week or so and found that Dan and I had a lot in common. He was training to get his pilot's licence, had done several skydives, ridden a little, and was an outdoor sporty guy.

We then had a chat on the phone. He was very quiet, nervous and quite hard work. Dan was not what I had expected from what he had done and achieved but I didn't let this put me off. Perhaps he would just take a while to get to know, which wasn't a bad thing. He had a Biology degree and worked in research, testing agrochemicals. He lived in Southampton, had recently split from a long-term girlfriend and was back living with his parents.

He was a huge distraction from my injury, and I felt very excited. Mum and Sue had always said I would find someone, but when I told them I was going on a date they looked awfully shocked. I think this showed they had really thought that I wouldn't. They had been trying to make me feel more positive about my future. Combined with the excitement was a huge dose of apprehension. What if he was lovely and then couldn't cope with my paralysis? What if I peed myself in front of him? To be rejected would be another knock to my confidence, which at the moment I really didn't need. It was scary but I didn't let that stop me, I decided to go for it and we arranged to meet up.

I told Dan that two friends would also come with me for this evening out. This was still only a year after my accident, and I needed help at times. I also felt safer with my friends. I got ready in the hotel in Oxford, where we decided was a good location to meet being roughly half way. Anna and I cracked open a bottle of champagne. I had a quick chat to Shane before I left. He advised me to go steady on the drink but I needed a fair drop to calm my nerves. We met in a funky bar in the centre of Oxford, and Helen also joined us there. I was wearing jeans with a smart top and I was sitting on a leather sofa with my chair hidden well behind the sofa.

I didn't get off to a good start. I hadn't noticed, but Dan had come in just as I was downing a shot of

Sambuca. I slammed the empty glass on the table to see him standing there, smiling. I apologized but he saw the funny side, luckily. The evening went quickly and we got on well. I even got a kiss. That was two in a month now. Perhaps this damned wheelchair didn't have the same effect on others as it did on Tim.

Anna had already helped me in the loo once, I just needed my jeans pulling up. It is difficult to do this when you can't get up off your bum. It was not unusual to go to the loo with your friend anyway, the perfect opportunity for a quick girly chat; I was a little embarrassed when we were about to leave the bar and I realised I had peed on the leather sofa. The two things that made this bearable were the effects of the Sambuca, and my friends.

Anna told Dan I didn't like to be watched whilst I got into my chair, even though I had already done it once earlier in the evening. Bless, he waited at the door. Anna and Helen then helped me into the wheelchair. I hated getting back in my chair. I had felt normal sitting on the sofa and I'd almost forgotten I was paralysed. Now, I felt self-conscious in the chair, pushing alongside Dan as we left the Bar, when I wanted to be walking alongside him in some sexy high heels, and wearing a dress, holding his hand.

Dan did not show any signs of being put off by the wheelchair, and he didn't know I had peed, so that was a relief. I had got away with it.

I couldn't believe it, he was keen, he wanted to see me again. This was like a dream. I pinched myself to check. I hadn't felt this happy for ages. Dan and I then saw each other every weekend. It was awkward for me at times because I needed to talk to him about catheterizing very early in the relationship; not exactly the sort of thing I wanted to discuss. In the end I plucked up the courage to tell him that I had to go every few hours and that I couldn't feel when I needed to, which meant that sometimes I got it wrong. Incredibly he was undisturbed by what I told him, and it was a huge weight lifted off my shoulders.

Dan made me feel special again. He made me feel attractive. I even started to wonder if my accident was as tragic as I'd thought. I had met a handsome man, who was also intelligent, sporty, and a talented piano player. The most important aspect in my life had picked up. I was so, so much happier.

The summer was spent riding Spark. I was hacking out and trotting on, but I didn't feel it was something I wanted to invest all my time in. I also knew I was vulnerable up there in the saddle. If I'd been enjoying it, I would have been prepared to take the risk, but as I wasn't gaining much from it I could not see the point of continuing. I couldn't imagine wanting to spend days at dressage shows; after all it had been my least favourite phase when I was eventing. I did go and watch the para-dressage riders train but I knew by then that it was not going to be my thing. All I would have to do would be a walk and trot dressage test; not my idea of a good day's sport. It was harder for me to take to it because only 18 months earlier my dreams were Burghley and Badminton. I decided to quit after a number of weeks of trying. How would I ever find something I loved?

I found my days were hard to fill. My exercises took up a fair few hours but I had not found a lot else to fill the rest of my time. I'd got into a pattern of getting up late, and sleeping as much as I could. This wasn't good, and it wasn't me at all. Before my accident my days were long and full. I realised that I still had a very long way to go.

There were still spells of down days, but then I would bounce back. I could not be in a new relationship and be depressed, that would be sure to ruin what I had got. When I was feeling like this I would send a text to Dan to say it might be best if he were not to come at the weekend. I was scared he would go off me if I wasn't in good form but he convinced me that he should still come. He was right.

When there was a hog roast at a local farm to raise money for Matt's trust, I asked a few friends, and a group of us went along. I started to feel as if I was eighteen again. Now that I'd started to enjoy parties and a few drinks I was losing my inhibitions and some of the awkwardness I still had about being in a chair. I knew that there was every chance that Tim would be there, probably with the new girlfriend he got with a very short time after we split up. He was. If I had not been so lucky as to have met Dan, this could have made me feel totally rejected, but thankfully, we had both moved on. I was very proud to be sitting next to my new boyfriend. I wondered if Tim would speak, and after his friends encouraged him to he did say a few words. I appreciated that. I found the break with Tim easy; very different from my split from Jonathan which took me a long time to get over. There were two reasons for this; first I'd had eight awful months knowing the break with Tim was coming, and second, he wasn't my best friend. The only thing I found it difficult to forgive Tim for, was the way he treated me in order to make me end the relationship, and, that he'd never once got in touch to see how I was coping. His presence there certainly did not spoil the night. We all had a really super time. I even rode the bucking bronco, slowly. Getting around at the end of the night was tricky; a broken glass on the dance floor had caused two flat tyres. Matt looked as though he'd had a great night too; our spinal injuries didn't mean we couldn't enjoy ourselves as much as everyone else – plus we always had a chair!

Dan must have thought I was a party animal who liked a fair bit to drink. It's true, I did like a good time but really I was equally happy with nights in. It was just that the first few months I was with Dan there were quite a few social occasions. I had been organising a fundraising auction at the family's 'Eye Kettleby Lakes' venue. This was suggested by a friend, Fiona Monteith, who had a lovely holiday house in Whistler, the perfect skiing retreat. She offered a week in the house as one of the prizes, if I wanted to organise an auction.

That was how it started. I spent a lot of time emailing local businesses asking for auction prizes and, once again, was blown away by people's generosity. Mum and Dad helped me send out the invitations for this 'champagne and canapés' evening. It was well supported and the money raised helped me get much of the equipment that was at Project Walk, and to continue to have two sessions of rehab a week with Kate.

Once again, I had fun. My smiles were not just on the outside; I felt happy from the inside. These days were coming more often now. The good days definitely started to outweigh the bad days. There were still occasions when I would have a dark day or two. When Bob was competing at Burghley or Badminton I was pretty much guaranteed to feel like rubbish. I did not go back to Burghley the second year after my accident but I did sit at home to watch it on TV. I loved to see my friends compete, many who had helped me through the tough times but when Bob and Jeanette were on I would still feel sick, not with nerves but with the pain. Alice Fox-Pitt was commentating on TV and she made me feel better by mentioning my accident and that I had produced Bob. I was so proud and I felt like I owned part of that horse.

Dan was very understanding, and handled the situation perfectly. He is a quiet person anyway. He was there for me but not trying to make me talk or laugh, he just accepted that this was a tough time for me. He popped out to the shop and when he came back I was lying on the floor still watching horse after horse wishing it was me competing. He placed some flowers next to me. "Rest in peace," he said. He'd made me smile on a day when it looked as if that would be impossible. I had huge admiration for how he coped on the days when I wasn't my usual self.

I still worked on my rehab day in, day out. I had a treadmill, a hoist and harness in the garage in which I would dangle from the roof. I had two people, usually my Mum and another friend on each leg and we would do assisted walking. The more I did the easier it got. Maybe this would trigger some improvement? It always made my back feel better, the movement in my lower spine felt fantastic, and so too did being stretched out.

If I spent a long time in my chair my back hurt. I started to show some positive signs. I could now feel backache and my feet were sweating again. Complete spinal injuries should not sweat from below the injury level. So the two improvements were smelly feet and lower backache – marvellous! I could also tighten my abdominals and obliques. My core strength had noticeably got stronger. Surely this meant that a signal was getting through the damaged spinal cord, and if I got a little bit of muscle function and kept repeating it, then maybe it would get stronger.

Dan and I had been getting on well, and been together for five months, when we decided we would go on safari in Kenya for a week. I used some of my savings as I thought I deserved a treat after the few months I had

had. The trouble with the injury though, is that it always comes with me, so a holiday felt impossible.

The doctors were horrified when I told them I had been. "What if you had a urine infection?" one said. I hadn't really considered the things that might go wrong, I just decided I wanted to do it and got it booked. It was a wonderful holiday in many ways. After all, it is not every day you see beautiful wild animals; it was pretty amazing. I felt guilty because I was lucky to be in one of the most stunning places in the world, yet I was desperate to get home.

The whole trip had been quite a big ordeal for me, and others must have thought this too, as one of the guests said: "What on earth are you doing here?" 'The same as you,' I thought to myself. We had three flights to get to our accommodation in the Masai Mara. I felt shattered by the time I got there. The change in my diet caused me to get the shits. Not good at the best of times but a nightmare with a spinal injury and definitely not great in a fairly new relationship.

The Land Rover ride out on safari was very bumpy and gripping on to the seat exhausted me. This was supposed to be a holiday and it was far from one. It could be frustrating and challenging when I was away, and it made me feel disabled. I so desperately wanted a holiday away from the spinal injury, or at least to take my mind off it, but my choice of holiday made this seem impossible, with the challenges being even more demanding whilst away than at home. Yes, the injury followed me everywhere and I wished it would just bugger off and give me some peace.

5

'Now, that does look like my kind of sport,' I thought to myself as I watched a clip of a monoskier on You Tube. I was eagerly trying to find a sport that I could fall in love with. I had been on four skiing holidays from the age of seven, but they stopped once I started secondary school. I really enjoyed it but never went again because all my time and money was spent on horses and eventing. Maybe my accident was starting to open new doors for me?

I looked into various options about how I could learn to ski. I came across a website for Disability Snowsport UK. I did not hesitate; straight away I sent an email to enquire about giving this sport a try. A fortnight later I had my first monoski lesson booked at an indoor centre at Castleford near Leeds. I somehow knew it would be for me, and for the first time in ages, I was actually feeling rather excited about finding an alternative sport to eventing.

When I watched para-dressage I know that my eyes didn't light up, but, they did when I saw the monoskiers. For me, there was no comparison; monoskiing looked fast, furious and crazy. Surely it would give me the adrenaline rush I'd been waiting for.

The day we had to go to Castleford couldn't arrive fast enough, Anna had also booked a lesson in a beginner's group, and we were going to make a day of it. Hopefully we would be enjoying a well deserved meal afterwards. I had bought myself some cheap ski clothes ready for the first lesson, which was going to be in a giant freezer with artificial snow. I had to wait for my instructor because we'd arrived slightly early. When a very good looking guy - yes, he was my instructor - came along, I felt he had been worth the wait. It was going to make falling over more bearable if I had him to pick me up each time. Dom introduced himself and explained to me the different ski options I had. The choice would be between two types of adaptive skis: a bi-ski, or a monoski. The usual advice would be mono-skis for injury levels T6 and below, and bi-skis for higher injuries. I was a T4 injury so based on that I should use a bi-ski, but Dom went on to tell me that we should also try a monoski, as you can be more independent, and ski to a higher ability.

It was no doubt going to be tough with very little core strength. Dom came back from the storage room carrying the heavy monoski. It had a small bucket seat and was on a single ski. For a fleeting moment I did wonder if I was totally mad. There I was paralysed from a risky sport, and now I wanted to learn to speed down a mountain with a plank under my arse. This just goes to prove that a spinal injury might damage your body but it doesn't change your character, or at least it doesn't have to. It was a relief to know that I was still me.

Dom explained a bit about how it worked, and showed me the two outriggers. They were like short crutches with little skis on the bottom and these would help me to steer. As it was my first lesson, Dom suggested that he should hold on to the back of the monoski and ski with me, to give me a taste of what it would be like once I had mastered the sport.

He pulled the straps very tight around my waist, chest and legs; I certainly wasn't going to come out. The monoski should feel like it is part of you, and so with any movement you make, the monoski should turn with you. Dom attached a special quick release mechanism to the monoski that hooked on to the drag-lift, and very soon we were both at the top of the slope. He took hold of my monoski and whoosh, we zoomed down. It felt ridiculously fast and exhilarating. Instinctively I just knew it was going to give me a real sense of freedom when I was doing this on my own. From this first moment I knew I had found a sport which would give me the same buzz as I felt when eventing.

We had several whizzes down the slope, and each time it would have been clear from the look on my face that I was going to be booking another lesson. Towards the end of the lesson I attempted a small bit in a straight line on my own, on a low gradient slope just enough to know it was not going to be easy. This though was the challenge I needed; it was what had been missing from my life since my accident. I was determined that I would get to grips with it, no matter how much effort and determination it took.

I was so disappointed when I heard that Dom was leaving Disability Snowsport and that he was off to the Alps to teach. Dom passed on the contact details of Rachel, another instructor, so I continued to have lessons at the indoor snow centre.

I tried to persuade Sue to try skiing. At first, she refused but in the end she gave in and said she would give it a go. She had always avoided it in the past because she had a history of knee problems but somehow I managed to persuade her to try just one lesson.

It was my fourth lesson and I was on the nursery slope, mainly lying on my side. Staying upright was near to impossible. It was frustrating. Sue could feel the tension from the balcony and she felt uncomfortable watching. I was improving though and all I could picture in my mind were the paralympic skiers. Throughout the hour I was on the slope I could hear this voice in my head, 'One day this will be fun. Bloody pull yourself together now...come on!' I managed to ski the whole nursery slope on my own by the end. I felt ecstatic even though I am sure it still looked pathetic.

It was then my turn to have a cuppa and watch Sue from the café upstairs. Sue's friend, Helga, was also booked in for a lesson. Helga got on quite well but Sue was comical. Sitting up on the balcony, I was doubled over with laughter as I watched Sue down below. I got some very strange looks. Sue didn't ski down the slope on her feet, she spent most of it with her knees bent and lying flat back on her skis. She ended up tangled in the safety netting at the bottom of the piste, and when the instructor tried to help her up she refused, shouting: "You won't be able to get me up!" But I noticed that, in the end, she had to accept his offer. It was clear that she didn't fancy staying in the freezer all night.

She looked at me a few times, with a fake smile and a wave that should have been the finger. I was crying with laughter. I went downstairs to meet her at the end of the lesson. She walked out with the rest of her group, carrying her skis, took one look at me: "I hate you," she said. Once again I burst out in hysterics. Poor Sue failed the first level, and what really aggravated her was that Helga passed.

Rather to my surprise, but also to my delight, before I knew it, Sue was booking another lesson. She was not going to be beaten. On the way home we both decided that learning wasn't going to be the best part of skiing, but if we stuck with it we could have some great fun, it had potential we agreed. The combination of extreme laughing and the exercise meant that I had a huge release of endorphins, and I felt really happy on the way home.

I'd been skiing every fortnight for four months and although I'd definitely made progress, I still wasn't as good as I'd hoped to be by then. I was still fairly useless.

I'd certainly not reached the stage of feeling the freedom yet, and I was nowhere near to reproducing that special feeling, the speed and the buzz that Dom had shown me in that first lesson. I would often fall, and as I couldn't get myself up I had to rely on my instructor. It was so frustrating, in some lessons I felt as though I had taken a few steps forward, and in others I felt as if I was going backwards and was worse than the previous time.

Again I was having a bad spell. I could feel that cloud descending and gradually enveloping me, but I made myself get in the car and drive to Leeds. I was living in hope that the ski lesson I had booked would be just the thing to lift it. After the two hour drive I felt lifeless and completely drained of energy. I couldn't get out the car and I hadn't enough fight left in me to struggle. Skiing required me to be in a strong mental state and full of determination; I was neither. I was frightened that one fall would send me into mental meltdown, and I didn't want to inflict this on my poor instructor, who would have to get me up. There was nothing I could do about it but to cancel the lesson and go back home. So, instead of this making me feel better, it made me feel worse - so completely useless and disappointed in myself.

There had been times like this before when I'd made myself do something and, as a result, I would feel better. This day had not been one of those days. When I had days like this, I felt like a failure. I often gave myself a hard time; I felt as if I was letting everyone down. Now when I look back, I know that I needed those days to enable me to come to terms with everything.

From the outside it looked as though my life was on track again, and of course it was in a lot of ways, but I still had the same problems too; these hadn't changed. I still had my bladder problem days and would have to suffer the embarrassment. I still had the days when my back would constantly ache, and the days when I would so hate the appearance of my body.

It was time for my yearly check-up at Sheffield Spinal unit. This included a bladder scan to check there were no stones, which is common with spinal injuries due to catheterizing. This check-up was very important as I wouldn't necessarily get any symptoms, I might not feel any pain. Everything was fine. The usual discussion with the doctor followed. The trip had certainly been worthwhile because he told me about a piece of rehab equipment that I might like to try. He knew how important exercise was for me, and he said it could be worth looking into. He quickly backed himself up by saying it would not return any neurological function, just in case he had given me some hope.

As soon as I got home I was on the internet looking for more information on 'Functional Electrical Stimulation'. FES is a technique that uses electrical currents to activate any nerves, causing paralysed muscles to contract. It was similar to what Hratch had done in his sessions, except this was 'functional', so the signals would be set up in a pattern that enabled my legs to pedal a static bike. The benefits were huge: increased bone density, increased muscle mass and tone, improved circulation. All of these would help prevent some of the complications we spinal injury patients can get such as pressure sores and fractures. Also the FES bike would give me a cardio work out; it would still be my muscles contracting and therefore I would need more oxygen.

This equipment sounded like a must have. I wished I had been told this whilst I was in the hospital instead of the fact my legs would waste. However it didn't matter, better late than never and to me this really was

88

important. I was on the phone to Anatomical Concepts straight away to get more information on these bikes and, of course, the price. Like all exercise specialised equipment it was expensive, but I was lucky, I could afford it thanks to my many fantastic friends plus help from the equestrian world.

The time it took before I could actually get going was the worst part. I had sixteen electrodes to stick onto my legs and bum, then I plugged them all in and strapped the legs on to the foot pedals. Not once though have I questioned whether it was worth the hassle.

Many spinal injured people suffer from pressure sores and can be back in hospital for months, some even have to have the area of damaged skin surgically removed. This is caused by having no sensation. Also, because the muscles are paralysed, the circulation tends to be poor in my legs so healing can be a slow progress. The FES bike not only built up my leg muscles but also my gluteus muscle. My bum was now a rounder shape rather than flat and boney. I continue to use this equipment five times a week and I would hate to be without it. This equipment should be more readily available to people with spinal injuries, and I am grateful to the doctor who told me about it that day.

Dan had not skied before, except for a one-off go on a dry ski slope years earlier. I had the perfect Christmas gift for him, a private lesson at Chill Factore in Manchester. I knew he would take to it like a duck to water and a group lesson would be too slow for him. I was right, as I had expected he was a natural.

These snow centres are ideal to learn the basics but they can't emulate the best factors of a ski holiday: the breathtaking scenery, fresh mountain air and the total freedom of being able to cover miles of pistes.

Dan and I decided that we would have a short holiday, and surprisingly Sue was up for it. Mum was a reasonably experienced skier and was excited to join us too.

I could keep going to these indoor snow centres for years and never be particularly good, but on actual ski holidays I would have all day to ski and the slopes were going to be longer, so I could just keep going.

My eventing clothes were still in the wardrobe. Up until now I couldn't bear selling them, it would have seemed like I was closing that chapter of my life. I had a top hat and tails for dressage, a body protector for the cross-country, breeches and jackets etc., and they were all worth a considerable amount. At last I felt in the right place mentally to sell them. I knew I was going to stick with skiing, so I posted them on Facebook to sell. I thought to myself, 'if I ever get back to eventing then I'll just have to treat myself to new gear.' The priority was to sell them so that the money I got for them could buy me some stylish ski gear for this holiday. I confess, I felt I deserved it. That was one shopping trip I really enjoyed!

I decided to go to a ski school in Morzine. I got in touch with them and I could book lessons but not hire a monoski. I was disappointed. I knew I needed lessons but I also wanted to do some skiing with my family and I needed my own ski to do this.

Ivor had given me money for flying lessons which I still had. I told him how I had found a sport that I was really determined to learn. Ivor is a keen skier and with no concerns he said I could spend the money on a monoski. I bought the same model as I had been learning on. I had not tried any different models, so had little knowledge, and I was in a rush to get a few days' skiing in before the season ended.

After the journey to L.A., the one and a half hour flight to Geneva was a real doddle. I didn't have to stress about having to go to the loo whilst flying. We hired a car and travelled to our hotel in Morzine. As we drove up the mountains it brought back amazing memories of family ski holidays from when I was a kid. I was tingling with excitement. I simply couldn't wait to get out on to the slopes.

Sue and Dan also had a lesson booked. Mine was with the ESF (the French ski school). I had a specialist adaptive skiing instructor named Jean-Fred. Over three days I learnt so much, but it wasn't without a serious struggle. I would have a rope attached to the back of my ski so Jean-Fred could try to prevent some of the falls, but that was only for a short time. I was soon on my own, and I had some real head-bashing tumbles. I knew I was making a meal of it but I was absolutely determined to master this crazy sport. Mum could see the fight in me had returned. It was the same as before my accident. Eureka, I had found my old self! It wasn't all plain sailing though, by a long chalk.

After one fall too many, I hit the snow with my outrigger in temper. "Right, I have had enough, come on – bloody well get on with it," I said under my breath, verging on tears of frustration. Jean-Fred pulled me up yet again and shouted: "Look down the piste, not at your feet." With total focus on each turn and maximum concentration I nailed it. I linked eight turns without crashing. I took a deep breath, a sigh of relief and a smile at last for Dan, Sue and Mum, who were all watching.

My ski lessons were in the morning, but I had not yet been up to skiing alone in the afternoon, as I'd hoped to be. On the last day I had a great morning and felt confident to try without the instructor. Dan, Mum, Sue and I went off on an easy run I had been doing. I couldn't bloody do it. I fell every two metres again. Dan would take his skis off, heave me up only for me to topple over again. Although Jean-Fred was teaching another lesson, he saw me and rescued me by skiing me back to the lift. I was so relieved to see him I could have kissed him. In hindsight I clearly wasn't quite ready for that challenge on that day, but sometimes you don't know unless you try.

Sue had now improved significantly and she was thrilled to finish the week uninjured. Well, that was until she tripped coming out of the sauna on the last night with a wine glass in her hand. Luckily she was OK except for her shoulder, which that she had jarred badly.

I'd been longing for this break from my spinal injury. A ski resort wasn't the most accessible place for me though, the doors tended to be too narrow for me to get in to the bathroom unless I was carried. Nevertheless, I did get away from my injury. Whilst I was skiing I felt like a real sportswoman again, although admittedly a rubbish one. The concentration took over, the will to crack it, the thrill from achieving it; all this took me away from thoughts of my paralysis. I was able to park those back with my wheelchair. It's impossible to describe that truly wonderful feeling. My self-esteem started to recover now that I had found a sport that I loved or, at least, I knew I was going to in the near future. Dan enjoyed it equally.

Over the next few days we weighed up whether we could afford another short trip over to Morzine. Little by little, I had started to discover that having a disability wasn't all bad. At the airport I didn't have to queue - ironic as I was the only person with a chair - and I got a free lift pass. Dom was going to be in Morzine so I could have lessons from him; these would be both cheaper and better. So we made the decision to have another four days before the season ended.

My aim was to be able to ski independently. This time it was just Dan and me. We stayed at the same hotel, and being familiar with the resort made it much easier. I had some fantastic lessons. Very soon I started to feel the adrenaline rush I had been waiting for. I was getting quicker now; being low down made it feel even faster. I was sometimes very close to a fall but mostly I was able to save myself; at other times I would lose it. This mixture of fear and excitement was the closest thing I could find to leaving the start box on a cross-country run.

I was having full days skiing and was shattered by the evenings. Dan and I were happy to relax back at the hotel and enjoy lazing by the pool-side. It was Easter time and the weather was glorious so we sat outdoors on the sun loungers soaking up the sun's rays whilst simultaneously admiring the snowy mountains.

Dan looked a little uncomfortable; he was certainly on edge about something. It wasn't much later when I saw he was holding a small box in his hand. He turned to me and, instinctively, I knew what was coming. In a soft but anxious voice Dan said: "Will you marry me?" I accepted of course; I would have had to be totally mad not to.

It wasn't even a year earlier when I had split from Tim. If someone had told me then that I would be engaged this time next year, to this very special man, I just wouldn't have thought it possible. You never know what is around the corner. The last day skiing was just my fiancé and me, and I managed it. We stuck to a slope we knew well. This was paradise. As I sat on the chairlift with Dan's arm around me, I glanced around at the blue sky and bright white snow, there were people having fun everywhere. How could I not feel lucky to be here right now with the guy I was going to marry?

Shortly after this second ski holiday, I went to visit Ivor who only lived ten minutes away. I took my ski photos to show him, told him all about the holiday and how amazing my new monoski was. The most important reason for my being there was to see how he was. He'd just had a nasty fall whilst skiing in Whistler, a holiday he'd bought at my fundraising auction the previous summer. A group of them had been away skiing including my Dad. Ivor had ended up in Vancouver hospital after fracturing his T4 vertebra and then having pneumonia. It was the same injury level as mine except Ivor had fortunately managed to get away with not damaging his spinal cord.

Whilst I was there with Ivor, he was on the phone to one of his friends, Gareth. He passed the phone to me and told me to have a chat with Gareth because he ran a ski holiday business, renting out chalets in Morzine. He asked about my monoskiing, and I found out about his accommodation. The whole afternoon was ski talk; it felt phenomenally wonderful to be looking forward to the future and to feel genuinely passionate about a new sport.

It was a couple of weeks later when I got a call from Gareth. He wondered if I would be interested in some part-time work in the office, his business was only a ten minute drive for me, just the other side of town. I was certainly interested so we met up to discuss it further. 'Simply Morzine' is a family business that was set up by Mike Marshall, Gareth's father. They run five chalets in Morzine. They had not had any help with the administration previously but they had recently taken on another chalet and had too much work.

I had never done anything like this before but it seemed a great idea, and with the possibility of some cheap or even free ski trips. There were of course worries. Could I use the loo in their house? Could I get in the office easily? What if I peed myself in front of these men? Ummm, that could be awkward; I would die. We arranged for me to do half days and they soon built a ramp for me to get in. For the first few weeks Gareth just helped me up the step. On one occasion I went flying, Gareth looked panicky but I reassured him that I was used to it, after all I ski. I did feel stupid though as I lay on the pebbles in a heap. He didn't want to get Mike to help. I think he was as embarrassed as I was, and he somehow lifted me back in my chair. We both laughed; I more than he.

The first eight weeks were just a trial so see if it suited both of us, and it did. I got to learn everything through the summer months, ready for the busy winter ski season. When the season got closer I started working five half days. I got to know the family who became firm friends and it did me the world of good. It had given me a reason to get up in the mornings, and even when I was feeling a bit down I would always go in to work. It was guaranteed to distract me and take my mind off any negative thoughts. I never thought I would be working in an office, but then I never thought that I would be paralysed. My life had taken a new direction completely, and although it would not be my dream job I did enjoy being there. I learned new skills and I gained a lot of confidence, just by leaving the house and doing something which was out of my comfort zone. It was a stepping stone to bigger things. I had always thought an office job would be boring, and in some cases it probably is, but not here. I soon felt like they were friends and less awkward about any pee accidents I was bound to have.

By this time I thought it would be a good idea to do another fundraiser. Matt's hog roast was so much fun the previous year that I decided to do one at Dad's farm in aid of the Matt Hampson Trust, Air Ambulance and 'Get Claire Walking' for my continued physiotherapy.

My friend Ruth and I planned the evening and we had a bucking bronco competition. I was excited about the evening. Mum and Dad worked hard to get the farm ready, and our local band 'Locked Out' kindly played for free. About 400 people came to enjoy the evening. It was going to be a cracking one; friends were arriving and drinks were flowing. For me it didn't last for long. I managed to have a go on the bucking bull, but I missed most of the night. I was embarrassed the next day to be told I was in bed by ten o'clock and I was unaware of anything. We'd been busy setting up all day and I had not eaten anything. Then once the evening started I was being given drink after drink, and rather foolishly I had knocked them back. I could go weeks without any alcohol so I could not handle too much. On this occasion it ended in disaster. I was being sick everywhere but refusing to go home. Henry had been on one side and Dan on the other to stop me falling out the chair. I kept grabbing the wheels and shouting: "No, I am not going, I will be fine." Eventually I was put in the car, driven back to the house by Dan and carried to bed. The little thank you speech I had planned, Matt had to do instead. "I wasn't supposed to being doing this but Claire is too pissed," he began. When the Leicester Mercury rang the next morning to do a report on its success I had to make up a story about how amazing it was. This was confirmed by the feedback I received, I had missed a fantastic night – bugger!

I had not felt this ill since being in intensive care. Much of the following day was spent trying to vomit but there was nothing left in me. From that day on I have been careful not to drink too much. It was shamefully horrendous!

When in the early days family, friends and even strangers had suggested things I could do with my life, not much appealed. At that time, I was spending too much time dwelling on what I had lost. As horses had been a massive part of my life for years, most of the ideas people came up with involved horses in some way. Dressage judging, driving, para-dressage, breeding and teaching were the common ones. I am the type of person who would love to teach but I was worried I would just feel envious that it was not me riding. That changed when, after almost two years, I was asked to teach a group. I made the decision to be brave and give it a go. If I felt fed up after then I wouldn't have to do it again. I half expected it to be the same as I found riding after my accident, but this was different. I got so much from seeing the riders improve. I actually got a buzz from it; it did not upset me in the slightest. I'd take the Quad-Bike to teach them from, and once again I succeeded in leaving my disability behind. I got genuine delight from seeing others do the sport I loved. For me, it felt more like eventing than simply getting up on a horse and riding again was ever going to. I had some lovely people to teach and afterwards, when they sent a text after a competition reporting on their success it always meant so much to me. It also gave me a reason to get outdoors again where I belonged.

Throughout the summer I combined teaching and working for Simply Morzine. There was less time now to think about what I had lost. Inevitably, it wasn't without a few low days, but on the whole I was starting to live life again.

When I became an ambassador for Spinal Research I wanted to fundraise for them. I felt inspired to organise a riders' fashion show after the memorable rugby fashion show I had been to. I thought this could make one brilliant night. I had never planned a fundraiser quite as challenging as this one but once I'd decided to do it I had to make sure it worked. It required me to put a lot of money in to it, more than I could afford. Yes, it was a risk but one that I had to take.

I spent hours emailing clothing businesses to see if they wanted to show-off their clothes. It was rather steady to begin with but by the end I had emails from more and more of them asking to be involved. In return I asked them to donate an outfit for us to auction after the fashion show. All the riders were brilliant and I soon got enough models including some Olympic riders. I was lucky to have found the help of a former event rider turned catwalk model, Laura Toogood. She was invaluable, organising the music and training the riders how to do the walk. This was as amusing to watch as the actual show.

The planning was stressful to say the least and selling tickets was a nightmare. I thought it was going to have to be cancelled and I would have lost £3000. People left buying their tickets to the last minute which is typical for any event. It was a job to know if I should go ahead, not helped by appalling weather that was putting people off. Hours were spent matching the riders to the clothes and making sure they had enough time to change. I ended up with over twenty different designers and around thirty models. The days leading up to it were when lots of tickets sold, and it started to look positive. I could breathe again. I found this the most gruelling event to organise, I had no idea just how difficult it would be.

It was held at Newbury Racecourse in a perfect sized room for the 400 guests, it looked impressive with the catwalk and lighting all ready for the models to strut their stuff. There was a lively atmosphere both behind the curtains where the models were getting ready, and when all the guests started to pile in. I had left plenty of drink behind the curtains for the models, as I thought some would need a bit of Dutch courage. I was in charge of running the event with friends and family helping with different jobs.

The fashion show part was now handed over to Laura. Mike Tucker was the compere for the evening. Both of them made it a fantastic night, as did all the models. It was noticeable how much drink was being consumed, as each time a model walked out she or he appeared to have savoured one more glass of wine.

My fears, sweat and stress were all worth it. It was clear to see what fun was had by everyone and in the process over £10,000 was raised. Half went to Spinal Research and half was going towards a hydrotherapy pool that I hoped I could afford to have in the future. Without these events it would have been impossible for me to keep going, to keep my focus and to raise the funds essential for further research into spinal injuries. The support was overwhelming and so many people with seriously busy lives had given up their precious time. I was touched by this and I knew I had no reason to mope about my injury. Life is what you make it. I could now start to see how many positive things I had going for me and how futile it was even to give a thought to the things I had no control over.

6

To most women the thought of their impending wedding day brings with it a feeling of huge excitement. For me, it was extremely worrying and filled me with so many concerns. I don't mean that I had any doubts about getting married to Dan, I most definitely had none. It was the thought of having to wear a wedding dress, of people taking photos of me in a wheelchair, wondering how on earth I was going to get down the aisle, worrying about whether my bladder would treat me kindly for once, and so many other lesser anxieties which had the tendency to magnify themselves in my thoughts.

As far as I could remember, I had very few photos of me in a wheelchair, if any, and I could not think of anything worse and more likely to make me feel on edge than photos being snapped all day. I'd have to be constantly checking if I was slouching, if I was round shouldered, if my feet were on the foot-plates or if I was running over them as they dragged along the ground.

I'd always had a penchant for fashion and my days at University in London involved a generous amount of time browsing in the designer shops and allowing myself a treat from time to time. I thoroughly enjoyed going to the occasional ball which gave me the chance to wear a posh dress. But things had changed and they were different now. The very thought of wearing a dress at any time, for any reason, these days, just felt ridiculous. It felt as if I was all dressed up but had wellies on still, the wellies actually being my chair. No, I could not wear a dress, it just would not go, it would not look right. So, what the hell could I wear for my wedding day?

I pondered over each of my worries in turn, hoping to find the answers. I would have loved choosing the right dress prior to my accident but not now. After numerous disastrous shopping trips just trying to find something casual to wear, I knew a wedding dress shopping trip would be a total nightmare. I would avoid this at all costs but I didn't even know where to start to find an option that I felt good about.

My other worry of how to get down the aisle, together with the thought of being made to wear a wedding dress and then wheeling myself down the aisle, made me feel sick. I would hate it, every one turning around to look at me. Again, my stupid body was depriving me of the day I was supposed to be looking forward to. Instead, it was turning it into a day I was dreading.

We had discussions and the only thing we could do was think of how to tackle these problems to make me feel as comfortable as possible. The photographer who took all the photos at the fashion show offered to do my wedding photos. Ian is a lovely guy. I felt very happy having someone I knew a little, someone I could talk to and explain what I wanted. We discussed using an attractive wooden garden bench for us to sit on for the photos, and shoving the wheelchair somewhere it couldn't be seen. I was beginning to like the sound of all this.

I got in touch with Gates Nurseries, our local garden centre which had already helped me by doing some fundraising. They very kindly offered to lend any of their benches. Dan and I went to choose one. Thank goodness, it was one problem resolved.

On the invitations we just asked for no photos to be taken. People possibly found it hard to understand why, as I hadn't minded any photos, or being looked at, when I was skiing, riding or doing something active. It was just to be seen sitting in the chair that made me cringe. Yes, I still felt unconfident about the way I looked.

The previous year I had been to Helen's for supper with a group of friends. Whilst I was there, I met a lady who made wedding dresses. She had a business in Shropshire. Lottie, an eventer and a mutual friend, told her that I was getting married and she sent me an email to say she wanted to help. As I read the first few lines my stomach turned, the thought of wearing a bloody dress was one I had just put clean out of my mind. However, I knew that the email deserved the courtesy of a response so I thought I had better at least discuss the options.

Hayley and I had a chat. She was understanding about my worries but also very persuasive and positive. Together we mocked up something we thought might suit me. I was still very self-conscious of my tummy; it was soft, flabby and stuck out. Sitting up tall and straight was difficult. I knew it was going to be impossible to look half decent but Hayley thought differently. I didn't want to spend a fortune on a dress I would wear only once and would probably dislike the whole time I was wearing it.

I gave Hayley my budget but she clearly wasn't doing this for the money. After several trips from Shropshire she would have been working at a loss but she insisted she would help. Hayley was just what I so needed. She made a dress with the stiffest corset she had ever made. I chose a pale pink coloured fabric with lace at the top and a small neat jacket to go with it. It was long but not too floaty so that it would not get tangled up in my wheels. Hayley was always confident that it would look great for my 'Big Day', and I had started to believe her.

When I tried it on, I was in definite need of reassurance, so I plucked up the courage to ask in a very weak voice: "Do I look fat in this? My tummy sticks out; it does, doesn't it?" "Shut up," came the response from Hayley, "I don't want to hear such rubbish again."

Hayley did make the perfect dress for me and what was even more remarkable about her was the way she handled this paranoid, stressed bride to be.

I didn't want the hassle of bridesmaids; I would have found it difficult to decide whom to have. But,I had two very special friends and it seemed quite obvious to me that I should have Henry and Shane as my 'bride's-boys' instead. Getting their suits was simple, just the one trip to the shop. 'It is all so easy if you are a man,' I thought to myself.

So, two sorted, it was now the last of my three main concerns I had to deal with. How would I get down the aisle? All of us had given it plenty of thought. We had even considered a Segway; maybe we could put straps behind my pelvis and in front of my knees like the standing frame I used. I think these electric stand-on balancing transportation devices take a while to get used to though, even for an able-bodied person. It was perhaps a daft idea and I could have ended up with a worse injury than I already had. It was just a fleeting idea, but it showed how desperate I was to get down the aisle without using my wheelchair.

The next idea was to use an electric quad bike. I was serious about this. It needed to be small so I got on to a website and ordered a kids' model. I was rather alarmed when it arrived and the box was so very little. When we got it out of its wrapping, we burst out laughing. I stood no chance whatsoever of being able to balance on that, and there was no room for my legs. Needless to say it was sent back. I was left scratching my head for another crazy idea.

Doing my research, I then came across a new pioneering robotic suit called the 'Rewalk'. I saw a clip online of this suit that enabled a paralysed man to walk again. "This is it – maybe I could get this in time, that would be totally amazing", I said in excitement to Dan. I emailed Rewalk but it was not yet available. I was told it wouldn't be long before one would be. Nevertheless, it had to be ruled out as an option for my wedding. By now I was losing any hope of finding a good idea.

We were getting married at Oakham Castle in the centre of the small market town. There was a playing field next to it.

I had a wonderful idea but felt it was unlikely to happen. I decided to try anyway; the worst I could be told was 'no'.

I sent Ivor an email asking him if he would be able to fly us to Oakham Castle in his helicopter. I was absolutely thrilled when I got his reply saying he was certainly willing to do this but, being as efficient as ever, he said he needed to check the area to make sure it was safe to land. First of all though, it was necessary to make sure that the relevant authorities would give their permission. If I managed to get their permission, then he would check to see if it was safe to land and take off.

I couldn't believe it when Rutland Council gave me permission. I told them I couldn't walk and didn't want to use the chair, so a helicopter would make my day. Even I thought my request was a bit optimistic, so I was thrilled when the answer that came back was 'yes'. Ivor soon carried out a recce of the venue and said it was possible. I was so relieved; at last everything was falling perfectly into place. It was topped by the fact that I would not even need to take my chair to the castle. I had two brides-boys, they could carry me. At last we had found solutions to all the anxieties that my injury had burdened me with.

I had decided where my 'hen do' would be not long after Dan had proposed to me. A few days' skiing would be the best hen trip I could ever wish for. I asked a few friends and their response was brilliant. I wasn't working for Simply Morzine at the time so I found a small chalet in Les Gets and booked it for eight of us. Dan obviously was not allowed to come on my 'hen do' and he was the expert on whom I had relied for helping me on and off the chairlifts, in and out of the monoski, and picking me up when I fell. This role for these few days was going to be Henry's, who as my Bride's-Boy was included in the party.

I don't know who was more nervous. The group was made up of a mixture of abilities, ranging from complete beginners to very competent skiers; I was somewhere in the middle. My friends had all the hen-do gimmicks with them and at Geneva airport I was given the bride-to-be sash and badges, but my favourite was the fluorescent green spikey wig. Lucy and Henry arranged these, and all eight of us had them. This was undoubtedly going to be a fabulous few days.

My friends had made such an effort to make it so memorable. They had been in touch with Dan asking him questions which I had to try and answer. I was told we were about to play this game and each time I got a question wrong I would down a shot of a drink of my choice. I was a bit apprehensive what the questions would be. My friends who had witnessed my drunken incident at the hog roast were quite kind and I got to nominate a friend to have the drink instead of me having them all. Understandably they didn't relish the thought of cleaning up my vomit after seeing the mess at the hog roast night.

We had loads and loads of laughs, and I had an amazing time with a few of the many friends in my life who had helped me get through some of the darkest of days. I appreciated all they had done for me over the previous three years to help me get to the stage where I was now, having the time of my life.

We had long days out on the snowy mountains in glorious weather, much piss-taking and plenty of speed, as we raced down as fast as we could. It was easy to spot each other with our wigs on, and we all looked pretty damn cool; well we thought we did.

On the first day I thought we were going to be in trouble when my chair went missing. We had returned from a great morning skiing to see Percy the chair had gone. "Where the hell is Percy?" shouted Henry. My wheelchair was named Percy quite early on after my injury, I couldn't quite stand hearing the word wheelchair as it was a word I never thought would apply to my life day in and day out. I had got to a point of accepting it, but his name had stuck.

Although I still hated him as much as ever, I knew that I relied on him, so I was understandably worried about where he had disappeared to. Friends were in the restaurants looking and asking staff where he was, but unsurprisingly got blank looks. It must not have been easy for them to take eight people with bright green wigs on seriously, but our faces all had the same seriously worried look. Eventually Percy was located. He had been put away in a garage with some others that belonged to a group from Belgium who were monoskiing here and they had thought that Percy was one of theirs. I had never been so pleased to see him.

We didn't have really late nights; you can have those anywhere. Here, when I had perfect snow conditions and sunshine, and beautiful mountains outside, I wanted to enjoy long days' skiing. We were out early every morning and we covered miles each day. Henry soon learnt how to pick me up after my falls, which of course I got abuse for. It was every bit as good as I had anticipated and we all went home in one piece.

I was immensely lucky to have five ski trips that winter and I was skiing red runs well. These are rated as difficult. I always came back shattered but having had a most brilliant time. The falls were getting fewer and I needed only limited help now. I was becoming fairly confident, that is until I fell off the edge of the mountain. Thankfully there was another piste running directly below.

I had lost control and was aware of the sheer drop so I deliberately tipped myself over but kept on sliding. 'Shit, bollocks and bugger!' I thought to myself when I realised I was not going to stop. Then I started to fall and to somersault down off the side of the piste. When eventually I stopped, I was so relieved to feel absolutely fine. I looked up to see the very anxious looks on the faces of both Ivor, who was on this ski trip, and Dan, as they peered over the edge. There were also other skiers who were stopping to see the crazy monoskier. I shouted up to them: "I can't feel my legs, I must be paralysed." We all chuckled but I was in trouble for frightening the lives out of Ivor and Dan.

I was someone who hadn't suffered from headaches until my accident and my spinal injury. Now they were a sign that something could be wrong and my body was trying to warn me.

For the past few hours I had been suffering from a headache and it was getting more severe. This one was much worse than usual; it was pounding so severely that I was in agony. I knew that I had to get back to the chalet as quickly as I could. At that moment I felt as if I might be dying. To make it even more unbearable I had to ski some moguls to get back, the ultimate torture for a head that felt it was about to explode.

I didn't say a word as we travelled back to the chalet; the pain was so intense I couldn't speak. I was sweating but I was feeling really cold. I went into the chalet and by this time, I was crying. Dan passed me a catheter and I had a very long pee. As the pee was emptying from my bladder my headache slowly started to fade and within a few minutes it had disappeared completely. It suddenly occurred to me what had happened. This was called Autonomic Dysreflexia (AD), something I had been told about in the hospital, and read about in the booklet.

AD is potentially life threatening and occurs in spinal injuries from T6 (two vertebrae lower than my injury) and above. It is a reaction of the involuntary nervous system to overstimulation. In this incident I think it was caused by a bladder infection. I had tried to catheterise two hours earlier but I thought there was no urine to empty. As a result the bladder had become too full and a blockage was possibly preventing the bladder leaking, so it kept filling. Headaches are a common sign of AD and causes the blood pressure to shoot up. It is dangerous because complications such as seizures and strokes can occur. I was very lucky because once I had an empty bladder I was fine. Again it made me think about the complications of spinal injuries, something I rarely did. I couldn't believe how I could go from extreme pain to feeling absolutely fine, and that I was so soon able to join the others in the chalet for a delicious meal.

I worried both my family and friends on several occasions whilst I was skiing, especially if there were any trees nearby or any severe drops, but the more experienced I became, the more I felt in control, and the less often they needed to worry. I loved this sport. I watched the skiers at the Paralympics and I couldn't help but be impressed. "I wonder if I could race?" I said to Dan. "Of course you could," he replied.

He always believed in me. I always enjoyed the thrill of competing when I was riding. I was sure this could be similar. I got in touch with the British Disabled Ski Team. Shortly after I was invited to go on a weekend course at Manchester's Chill Factore for an assessment, and possibly be offered a place onto the Development Squad.

The weekend was in August, just after our wedding day. I looked forward to giving this my best shot and perhaps becoming one of the best monoskiers in the country.

What a fantastic winter it had been, there had been less time to think about being paralysed, and I always had a ski holiday not too far away to look forward to. I was religiously sticking with all my rehab, and did not feel guilty when I was away skiing. Nor should I, because this was one of the best ways for strengthening my core. I controlled my monoski using my hips, and my core was certainly getting stronger as a result. Kate could see the improvements. In fact, any one could. As I lay on the floor I could tighten my abdominal muscles. There was a signal getting through my injury level. I was diagnosed a complete T4 spinal cord injury yet I could now contract muscles down to my hips. Maybe I could improve further; I was certainly going to keep trying. It was easy for me to know how much happier I was now by how fast the time was flying by.

It was already time for another trip to Sheffield for a bladder scan, an x-ray and to see the consultant. The first year had felt like an eternity but the past year, particularly the last six months, had zoomed by. I got on the bench for my scan, Mum was with me. "Is there any chance you could be pregnant?" asked the nurse.

Shit, what should I say? There was a chance, but if I was I would be only three days pregnant – unlikely, I thought. I wanted children but wasn't expecting it to happen so soon or that easily; after all I have only one ovary. There was a short pause before I answered, "No." Mum was looking at me and if I had said yes not only would she have fainted with shock, but she also would be left wondering if I was. In all probability I would then have to tell her in a few days' time that I wasn't, and she would be left wondering if I was trying for a baby. I didn't want that. The bladder scan was done and everything was fine.

It was only four days later when I felt different, but I questioned if you could really know that quickly. I did a pregnancy test and it was negative but I still knew I was. Maybe it was a bit early for it to show on a pregnancy test so I waited a few more days. It was a different result the second time. Even though I was sure it would read positive I was still in shock, along with Dan. I was worried. Perhaps I had been foolish. Did I really either want or need the responsibility of a baby?

My life had been so much better in the past few months. I'd received my assessment date to try to get selected for the Development Squad. Dan wasn't yet living with me, I still lived with my parents. My rehab would be affected; I might struggle to do anything at all once I got huge. The reasons for not having a baby formed a long list in my head. Dan was concerned too.

He was worried it could set me back. He had seen me go from strength to strength. I told a few of my closest friends. Selena sounded shocked at the thought of me not having this baby. I knew so early that all I would need is a little pill to terminate the pregnancy. Selena was a mother and was thinking I might live to regret this. She made me think again, and I decided she was right. I discussed it with Dan. Although our situation was not ideal, it would not be the end of the world. Imagine, we said, if we decided not to have this baby and then struggled to have one in the future, how agonising that would be. My heart was delighted at the thought of being a Mummy, but my head was screaming, 'Have you thought this through?' Yes, I was wondering how I would cope, and I was scared in case I was going to have any more dark days but these were few and far between now. Perhaps I could manage, and I knew my family would help me.

Mum and Dad were surprised when we broke the news to them. Although they knew I loved kids I think they thought I would never have a baby. They certainly hadn't expected to be given this news so soon. Mum wasn't sure she wanted to be a Granny yet, she said it made her sound old, but Dad was delighted. I wasn't planning on telling anyone, except it was hard to cover it up. From about four weeks into my pregnancy I started to feel this 'morning sickness' I'd heard so many people moan about before. It certainly wasn't just morning either, it was all day long. It was worse than I had ever thought.

I was still going into the office and feeling shockingly awful but, thankfully, I never was sick at work; just frequently at home. I couldn't believe Mike and Gareth didn't guess, I loved endless cups of tea and suddenly I'd gone off tea. I never ate biscuits or anything whilst in the office, as I was always watching my weight, and now I was snacking in an attempt to take away the nauseous feeling. It is a fact that I felt quite low during this time. Every day felt endless and I felt so sick that even working on my laptop became too much for me; sometimes I just had to lie still.

My wedding day was looming but I couldn't feel any enthusiasm whilst I frequently had my head in a bucket. My boobs had already grown and I was convinced by the wedding day I would be bursting out of Hayley's beautiful fitted dress. I could only do minimal rehab because I was so ill and missing it was awful, I needed to keep my body moving. Why was growing a baby making me feel like death? I expected that a tough pregnancy lay ahead, and I hoped this baby would make it all worth it.

The week leading up to our big day was worse than the previous three. Not only was I being sick, I'd also got a rather unattractive rash. It started on my stomach and was growing. I took a trip to the doctors because by now I was starting to panic. They didn't have a clue what it was. However I was given some medication to help the sickness on the wedding day. The rash had started to spread onto my arms and neck. "Bloody great!" I shrieked in despair when I looked in the mirror. I concluded that maybe I was allergic to getting married.

The night before our wedding day some of my good friends and I stayed in one of my parent's Holiday Lodges. We were in a 5-star Lodge called Cedar; it had a sauna, hot tub and a touch of luxury. We had an evening of pampering, chatting, laughing and checking to see if my face had a rash all over it yet.

I shared a room with Henry, who gathered I was pregnant when he had just nodded off to sleep and I squawked: "Get me a bucket... now!" He knew I had been feeling ill recently and so did other friends but I got away with blaming the frequent urine infections I'd been having. This actually was true. Although I had an appointment at the hospital to have my bladder flushed out, they wouldn't do it now that I was pregnant.

Urine infections are dangerous in pregnancy and can cause a miscarriage, so early on in my pregnancy I was put on a low dose antibiotic. I wished I'd been prescribed these a few years ago. To have stopped my having UTI's was a relief and it made life very much easier.

Now that Henry and Shane knew I was pregnant, they would understand why I was sick in the helicopter, if that were to happen. By then, I think I would have had to give in anyway. Luckily, the anti-sickness pills helped enormously, and when I woke up in the morning Henry checked my neck and face for the dreaded rash. Of course, as always, he had to try to wind me up. The good news was that my face was fine but my neck and arms looked blotchy; this didn't matter quite as much because I could keep my jacket on so it wasn't noticeable.

On the actual day, I felt quite calm. All my worrying had been done, everything was sorted and what would be would be. We had a long morning getting ready, sipping champagne and relaxing outside Cedar lodge on the loungers. I could not believe that today was the day I would be getting married, the day when really I should be walking down the aisle. But today that wasn't an option for me.

Melanie, my hairdresser, who was also a good friend, came to Cedar to do my hair; I didn't have to worry about that. Melanie knew me so well; I knew she would do my hair exactly how I'd like it. She certainly didn't let me down, but for further reassurance I asked both Henry and Shane; I knew I could always trust them to tell me the absolute truth.

My friends left Cedar to go to Oakham Castle. My two handsome Bride's-Boys were with me and, my goodness, I needed them. Between the three of us we squeezed me into the dress. It wasn't easy and we had to take such care so as not to ruin Melanie's hair styling. There were so many buttons on the back of the corset part of the dress, it was fiddly. I leaned forward over the bed, Shane prevented me from sliding off whilst Henry bent over me to do up all the buttons. It was just another reminder that the most basic things can be a struggle when you are paralysed, but it did cause us to laugh. Thankfully Ian, the photographer, had departed. It took me less than five minutes to do my own make-up. I was never keen on having too much of the stuff on my face and I saved some money too.

Henry and Shane looked absolutely gorgeous in their suits. Poor Henry had a small cut on his finger and when he was dressing he dabbed some blood on the collar of his white shirt. A minor disaster but nothing that a bit of white nail varnish wouldn't hide. Lucky we had it, one of the girls had left it in Cedar after doing a French manicure.

I heard the helicopter arriving and the next thing I heard was the panic in Shane's voice. Naturally I thought there had been some kind of disaster, maybe Ivor had made a bad landing or there was a problem with the helicopter. But no, it was much worse than that, Shane couldn't find his sunglasses. A major search around the Lodge and they were found. We all jumped in my car and drove over to the field where Ivor had landed. It was here where the marquee was set up.

I started to count my blessings. It was a phenomenal treat for me to be on the way to my wedding instead of to Nottingham Queen's Medical, where I had been the previous two times I was in a helicopter. My glamorous Bride's-Boys, both wearing sunglasses, got in the back two seats and I sat next to Ivor, who was also looking impeccable. We were ready for take-off.

It was less than ten minutes later when we could see all our guests gathering outside Oakham Castle. I felt overwhelmed with emotion. I gulped and had to fight back the tears. We landed smoothly and the boys carried me out. I had Henry on one side and Shane the other. This caused me to be a little lopsided as there is a big difference in their height, but Henry didn't want his feet to be chopped off to equalize things; I was not sure he was a true friend after all!

They carried me successfully into the castle and I sat in the chair next to a petrified but very handsome looking Dan. He was sweating and he told me he hadn't been able to eat breakfast, so I knew how nervous he was feeling. He was dreading having to make his speech, and had been for days. At least I think that is what it was, unless he was just starting to realise what a challenge he was taking on by marrying me.

Oakham Castle was a truly stunning venue. Ours was a civil ceremony, therefore fairly short. To our relief, neither of us made a mess of our words which we were both convinced we would. I had watched 'Four Weddings and a Funeral' too many times.

I was now Mrs. Claire Spincer and felt all grown up for a few minutes. My husband carried me out after all our guests had left the castle. One lady in Oakham who was watching me being lifted into the helicopter thought it was all very sweet. "Ahh, bless her, she doesn't want to get her shoes dirty," she said. Having no chair in sight was a fantastic feeling. Ivor took Dan, Doug, Dan's best man and me back to the marquee in the helicopter, stopping off at Ivor's house on the way.

I couldn't stop staring at my ring. How had my life gone from moments of wishing I had died in that fall to being married to this wonderful man and being pregnant with our baby, only three years later?

Dad called to say everyone was back at the marquee and we could set off again. All our guests were waiting outside as we flew in. There was a loud cheer to greet us as we got out, and this time I was lifted into Percy. I did feel awkward to be in the chair again, especially having to struggle across the grass but, thankfully, I was soon distracted and chatting to so many friends.

By the time we got there it was 5 o'clock. We'd decided we didn't want a daytime celebration followed by a separate evening party, so decided to make it just one big party and for it to be fairly casual. It was a hog roast with delicious salads made by a local caterer. It was followed by a scrummy authentic ice-cream cart, with all the best flavours and toppings or brownies available. I had been so looking forward to the ice-cream cart, but having had so many conversations with as many of our guests as I could, I got to the cart too late; it had been such a success that our 'greedy' guests had eaten my favourite mint choc-chip flavour, the same happened to Dan.

Dad and Dan both exceeded expectations with their speeches. Dad said some lovely things; I couldn't quite believe it was about me. When it came to Dan's turn he didn't appear to be at all nervous. I shed a few tears but soon stopped when I gave the gifts to the mums and my 'Second Mum', Sue.

The evening was perfect. It was exactly how we'd wanted it to be. The lovely wooden bench had been ideal for Ian to take some photos. Of course, when the band started to play I wanted to dance, I missed not being able to, but it was the only thing I found hard. Dan was probably relieved. We are different in that way; I could have danced the night away, he would have preferred to stay far away from it. Well, at least he would have tried to, but if I'd been on my feet he would have been dragged over there.

We spent a few days in Norfolk after our wedding day. Not exactly surprising that most of it was spent feeling sick and exhausted. I relaxed when I could, I lay by the pool and I also had a massage. Not all bad though because both Dan and I agreed that a ski trip the following season would be our real treat.

117

The Skiing Development-Squad selection weekend was soon here, but the sickness persisted. I had a few pills left so I saved them for this weekend. I was very aware that my life was going to change again very soon but I wanted to go on this training weekend, just to see what was possible.

There were talks in a function room about the Squad and what would be expected of everyone, followed by time on the slope. I sat and listened to the commitment involved, absorbing it all. It brought back memories of my eventing days. My life had taken a new direction now and, even if I had not been twelve weeks pregnant, I'm not sure that this would have been for me. Any sport at a high level requires total commitment and this usually makes you quite selfish. You have to give it your total dedication to achieve the best results you can, and after the interlude that I wanted to put behind me, I was now enjoying having a more varied life, and enjoying a new sport but in a less serious way.

I couldn't enjoy the skiing any more than I do when I am skiing with Dan, Mum, Dad, Sue and friends, so why change this? That is what I sat there thinking. Had I been ten years younger, it would have been very tempting, even though I had fallen in love with another expensive sport, and training would mean months away from home. The skiing there went well and I was offered a place on the Development Squad. I didn't take it.

My priorities were now Dan and this new little person, so it was not going to be possible or what I even wanted. I had also really enjoyed fundraising, so I could do more of this in the future and this would help many others. My recovery was now much further advanced than it once was, my personal despair no longer ruled supreme; I no longer needed to get sucked into focusing

Riding my first pony, Mickey.

Playing with my brother.

An early skiing experience.

My first year at Stamford High School.

Clive Dunn at the Pony Club Championships 1993.

My junior ride, Rodwell Grey at Poplar Park 1996.

Roland enjoying the cross-country at Hartpury 2005.

Roland at Gatcombe 2005.

Finishing my dressage on Bob at Hartpury 2003.

Bob in full flight at Pau 2006.

Above:
Loving the buzz, sky diving
from 14000ft in Australia.

Left:
Having fun in Sydney.

Left:
All ready to
hit the town
with school
friend Jodie.

Right:
A night out
just months
before my
accident,
with friends
(L-R) Selena,
Lucy and Anna.

Above & left:
My days at Project Walk
in California.

Below: Working with
Hratch on my rehab.

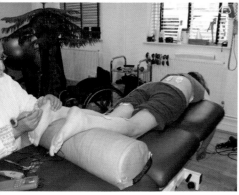

Back in the saddle, riding out with Henry.

Attempting a new sport.

I finally mastered mono-skiing after many frustrating lessons.

The perfect hen party in Les Gets.

Our wedding day with my Brides-boys and Dan's Best Man
(L-R) Shane, Henry and Chris.

Arriving in style.

Dan and Henry carry me back to the
helicopter. No chair in sight.

Sharing a laugh with Lissa.

With friends (L-R) Lucy, Ruth and Hannah.

*The most special gift
you could ever wish for.*

*Maisie enjoying a ride
on Raptor, Dad's bull!.*

Maisie changing my life.

The build up to the start of the Virgin London Marathon 2012.

Encouragement from Susanna Reid.

The very first step over the start line.

Above:
Matt Hampson
provided
the inspiration
I needed.

Clockwise:
Maisie supporting
Mummy.

Ben Fogle
supplying
some energy.

Tim Henman and
his wife Lucy
supporting my
efforts.

Half way point
at Tower Bridge
battling the rain.

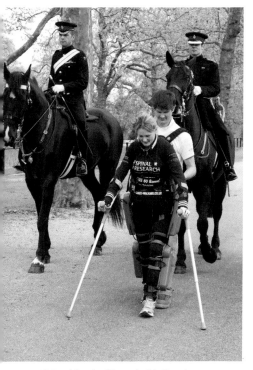

Joined by the Household Cavalry.

Paying our respects to Claire Squires.

The finishing line surrounded by supporters - A welcome sight.

Hugs from Dan and Dad.

*Presented with a box full of medals
by Matthew Pinsent.*

Sharing a joke with Dan.

Feeling the nerves before lighting the Paralympic Cauldron in Trafalgar Square.

Meeting David Cameron.

PA.

A moment of pride.

Celebrating the marathon success in my home town,
Melton Mowbray with (L-R) Maisie, Mum, Barbara , Kate and Sue.

Dan and I enjoying a party with Sir Richard Branson
at his London restaurant , The Roof Gardens.

Training throughout the cold winter days.

Maisie finding the cycle challenge rather exhausting!.

Talking to a secondary school and demonstrating Fred.

Leaving a primary school after my visit.

Greeted by Maisie at the finishing line.

*Joined by Melanie C, Dan Lobb
and Helen Fospero.*

Wonderful support from the celebrities.

Family and friends at the end of the cycle.

on myself. I knew that I wanted to do things that would help to change other people's lives for the better.

Immediately after the Development Squad assessment was the twelve-week pregnancy scan. It was during that scan I first felt the immense excitement and joy of pregnancy, when we saw our little baby. I now told all my friends. I sent a text, 'I know you thought I was a virgin at my wedding, well I am sorry to tell you that you were wrong, I am 12 weeks pregnant'. My friends were over the moon for Dan and me. It was at this point when reality hit. In seven months' time, I would be a Mummy.

I was genuinely excited about the baby but I also worried if the later stages of the pregnancy would make things even more difficult. I was a dead weight from the chest down, and now I had the extra weight of a baby. How would my arms cope? Would I be able to get in and out of the shower chair? How about the car? I had to do everything I could do, to keep fit, to prevent having too much extra weight to carry, and to stay busy so I didn't slip into depression.

Not surprisingly I started to think that maybe a few days skiing would be possible. I could wait and see how I was feeling, but if I went on the first week of the season I would be thirty weeks pregnant. Mike and Gareth were happy for me to decide at the last minute and this gave me the incentive to keep doing all the boring exercises.

The other thing I decided was to find something I could do during the later stages of pregnancy, so I found a jewellery-making course. When I was a child I had always liked being creative so I decided to try this evening class. I dragged Sue along to do yet another thing she never dreamed she would ever do. We did enjoy ourselves. I learnt lots, and we always had fish and chips after the class, that made it even better. I had a skill that I could use in the future, or if I didn't, at least I could make some presents for friends now.

I made the ski trip. It was a really fantastic week with Dan, Sue, my friend Bec, her boyfriend and her brother. I felt great and I wasn't struggling with my transfers at all. Of course I was cautious, and I limited my skiing to easy runs. The six of us chilled in the evenings and we all had early nights. In fact it was a competition as to who would go to bed first, just what I needed on this holiday.

I felt the baby kicking; I didn't know if I would, so I was thrilled that I did. It may have been different to what other women feel but any sensation to me was a bonus. I had chosen the hospital I was most familiar with, the Nottingham Queen's Medical Centre, to have our baby. I had a few trips there to meet the midwife and to form a birthing plan. A spinal injury 'mum-to-be' was something different for them so they found it quite interesting. My midwife did have some experience though and she seemed very knowledgeable. I had read that other women who had children after a spinal injury had them early. After the midwife and I had discussed possible birthing plans I asked: "Why are spinal injured patients more likely to have their baby early?" in a curious voice. Ideally I would like this small person to arrive at about 38 weeks. She replied: "It is because of urine infections, these can trigger labour and, because of catheterizing, you are more susceptible to a UTI". I smiled to myself. Now 36 weeks pregnant, I had a plan.

7

Swallowing the last antibiotic pill I would be taking for a few days, I thought to myself, 'This will be brilliant if it works'. I waited just forty-eight hours before I tested my urine with a 'dip stick'. Yes, the results showed that leukocytes were present indicating I had a urinary tract infection. I smiled to myself, and waited to see if anything happened.

A UTI can cause inflammation and bladder spasms, which can irritate the uterus and cause contractions. Thirty eight weeks pregnant would be a perfect time for the baby to arrive. The baby is considered full term from 37 weeks so it was safe for the small person to enter the world. If my plan was a success it would save me getting any larger, and everyone had told me it would be the last few weeks that would drag.

The following evening I was sitting on my bed reading a book. When I glanced down I noticed a wet patch, it was different to pee. I was now convinced that the urine infection had given the response I wanted; my waters had broken. I immediately rang the midwife and she told me to go to the Queen's Medical Centre first thing the following morning, unless I became aware of contractions, in which case I should go in during the night.

I didn't sleep at all that night. Adrenaline was pumping around my body, I was excited about my baby arriving and I was constantly feeling my lower abdomen to see if I could feel any tightening. Dan was away working in Southampton but I didn't want to tell him yet as it was unlikely it would all happen quickly. I was right. I went to the hospital in the morning but, as I expected, was sent home. I had been examined, my front waters had broken and this meant that I would be induced within twenty-four hours if nothing happened naturally.

I was able to feel the contractions as they became more intense. I was delighted as no one knew if I would be able to feel them or not. I had been worried about the lack of sensation. In some ways I felt lucky after the stories about childbirth I'd heard but I was equally upset by the thought of having little or no sensation. It was yet another time when I would feel disconnected from my body, seeing someone touch me and move me but if I closed my eyes I would be totally oblivious to it all.

It was time to go back to the Queen's Medical with my bag of clothes for the new baby and me. I was now back taking my low dose antibiotic, the mild UTI had done its job and I didn't need it anymore. My usual midwife, whom I had got to know, wasn't working so I was given a different one named Kathryn.

Straight away I liked Kathryn; we clicked and got on brilliantly well. She'd had no experience of spinal injuries but was exceptional in the way she made me feel at ease. She had a gentle, kind way but also she was fun. She broke my hind waters and then it was a waiting game. Hours and hours ticked by. It felt like a long haul flight wondering how much longer. I told Kathryn I felt as if I was on a flight to New Zealand. We decided she was the trolley dolly as she was excellent at bringing us refreshments.

Dan arrived, Mum was also with me, and Sue popped in for a short time. It was a relief to Dan and Sue that there was a Costa shop in the hospital with a good supply of cakes. My contractions were getting stronger but when I said they were taking my breath away, Dan, Mum and Sue just laughed, they were all so pleased for me that I could feel it. Of course I was too. I had to text Henry: "Thank god for spinal injury, even I can feel this so it must bloody hurt!"

It was a painfully slow night, but eventually Kathryn announced, in an ecstatic voice, that I was 10 cm dilated. It was all going well, I had powerful contractions. I got it into my head that it wouldn't be long until the baby arrived. I was seriously proud of my broken body; it wasn't letting me down for once. It was working, trying its very best.

The next time Kathryn checked was not such positive news. Her head was down but the back of her head was against my spine, making it difficult to push her out. The doctor scanned me to see if Kathryn was right and unfortunately she was. Things were not going quite so well, after all. I was gutted when I was told I would need an emergency caesarian section. "This is the worst day of my life. OK then, the second worse, or perhaps the third or fourth - a bad day!" I said, devastated.

I had been asked dozens of times if I would have a C-section because of my injury. The answer was no. For once in almost four years I was starting to feel pleased with what my paralysed body could do. My reasons were understandable. Having a C-section was going to be a nuisance. I wanted to get back into the rehab as soon as possible and I would now have to take it easy which is impossible when even a transfer on to the loo requires a decent effort. Another worry was how long they would keep me in hospital; I didn't want another night in one of these places. I had too many memories of some traumatic times. All these thoughts were rushing around my head, I was shattered now and it felt like I had been told the worst news, which of course it wasn't, by far. They discussed trying forceps delivery but decided against it, and at this point I just wanted to get on with the C-section. The sooner they started, the sooner all this would be over and done with.

I had to have an epidural. That may seem strange when I had no sensation anyway, but my body still feels it and can cause the life threatening Autonomic Dysreflexia. The next hour was hideous. I had an anaesthetist who clearly had no understanding of spinal injuries and he had an attitude that left a lot to be desired. He could not grasp the fact that sitting on a bench keeping very still with relaxed shoulders and a soft curve in my back was near impossible. He was also very rude to me and in hindsight I should have told him to bugger off and to get someone decent. The trouble was I didn't know if there was another way of doing the epidural and I certainly couldn't risk Autonomic Dysreflexia, so I allowed him to keep stabbing me with the needle in an attempt to find the epidural space. He did not seem to be taking care at all. By this time I was sobbing and almost collapsing with fatigue, but Kathryn kindly helped my body stay upright by placing her hands on my shoulders. My legs were balanced on a stool. I was shattered! This was by far the most intense hour of rehab I had ever done and I was an emotional wreck.

In the end he gave in and another anaesthetist entered the room, calmer and softer in appearance. He asked me to roll on to my side and to lie with my knees flexed in a foetal position. He managed to do it on the first attempt. If only I'd known it could be done so easily an hour ago.

The C-section took forever as well. I just tried to switch off. I felt as if I was freezing due to the drugs and the effect of my spinal injury on temperature regulation. I was shaking so much that my shoulders became unbelievably tense. I was in pain. I hoped this baby was worth all this. After Kathryn had given her a little clean, I was passed my tiny baby girl. I preferred my blood to be wiped away. It was amazing but I was shattered, drugged up, emotional and although I thought my little girl was beautiful, it took a little while for it all to sink in. Dan cuddled our 6 pound 3 ounce little miracle and it took a short time for us both to realise we had just been given the most special gift in the whole world.

I didn't rest much throughout that day. It was only 10 o'clock when my friend Lucy popped in for a drink. She didn't know that I had only just given birth when she texted me, but I asked her to pop over. My blood pressure was very low and was being monitored. I had lost a lot of blood. Typical of me though, I just carried on like I would have on any other day. I didn't realise actually how desperate I was for some sleep.

Dan and I discussed names. I was keen to name our little girl Maisie, after a wonderful lady who used to look after me when I was a child. She'd recently had a stroke and I'd been visiting her in hospital. I was so sad when she passed away before she'd been able to meet our Maisie. I had told her that I was pregnant when I went to see here, and that if we had a girl, I would love to name her after her. She said that she would be really honoured. I was very lucky because Dan loved the name, so we agreed that she would be Maisie Spincer.

Throughout the day, I held her close. I looked at her and admired her, but it wasn't until that evening, when I was left alone with her, that my heart melted. I was in my room and our tiny baby was in a small cot. She cried, and although I knew I had to be very careful picking her up because of the C-section wound, I carefully reached out and lifted her back into my arms. She stopped crying, she was content, and she was mine!

"Shit, I think she likes me," I texted to both Mum and Dan. I felt enormous amounts of love for her; I was totally overwhelmed by this little treasure. I kissed her forehead and tears rolled down my face, tears of complete joy. The sickness, the labour and the birth, they had all been worth it. This was magical!

The next couple of days were spent in the hospital, and Dan could stay too. They had to check everything was well and as it should be with Maisie, and as my balance may have been affected, that I could manage my transfers easily. I sprang up, because I now felt so light by comparison with how I'd been. Everything felt easier; I felt great.

All the nurses were so kind to me and my worries of staying there proved to be unwarranted. Of course, I was still pleased to be discharged, to go home with Dan and our precious little girl. I managed to drive us back home; it wasn't a problem, I had hand controls, and now I was feeling well again.

We had loads of visitors and Maisie was being absolutely spoiled as she was showered with the cutest clothes, teddies and gifts. I had never experienced anything like this; I was so content doing what seemed like nothing. Hours, every day were spent holding her and admiring her. To me, it seemed like only a very few minutes, this was a new experience and very unusual for me.

My Mum and Dad were delighted to have their first grandchild. Dad was actually skiing when Maisie was born, and he duly celebrated her arrival whilst he was away. His face when he met her for the first time said it all.

It was time to remove my staples. The midwife arrived at the house. To me, the wound didn't look fully healed but the midwife, again someone with no experience of spinal injuries, insisted it would be fine; who was I to argue with her?

It was impossible to go through the day without twisting and turning; even when I got in the shower or sat on the loo I had to pull my body with me. I would lift my bum onto the seat and then lift my legs to follow.

So it didn't surprise me at all when, by the afternoon, the whole wound had split open. It looked just like a letter-box. Thankfully for once I couldn't feel a thing, but it was a truly gory mess and I couldn't face looking at it.

Mum took me to the Doctor's Surgery, whilst Dan looked after Maisie. The doctor was quite worried and I was offered plastic surgery if I wanted it once it had healed because it could possibly leave a step in my tummy. He prescribed some antibiotics to prevent infection, and sent me home with lots of dressings. A few days later he even rang me to see how I was.

Mum was brilliant at dressing wounds; her years of experience with horses had made her an excellent nurse in circumstances such as this. The wound went on to heal well and I was very relieved to get back into my rehab routine quickly. It was not a choice, it was absolutely essential for me to keep my body fit and healthy. It was also vital I pushed on in order to make any possible improvements.

Becoming a Mummy was undoubtedly the most special time in my life. I had never experienced anything even close to this. It genuinely changed me. Maisie was top of the list now. For instance, I found I was far less bothered about things like a soft tummy, now that I had the most important role I ever had in my life. All my priorities had dropped down a place or two.

I had known that some things would be more difficult for me than for able-bodied mums, but once Maisie was born I never gave these much of a thought. I found a way to do most things, and with Percy's help I could push her pram around the house. It was a time consuming task but that didn't matter. I was just so chuffed that I could do it. With plenty of practice I got significantly faster. I was so so lucky to have Maisie in my life, and that was all I could think about.

To change her nappy, I had to lift my own body on to the bed; this was the only way possible for me. If I forgot the wipes or the nappy or milk, then even this supposedly simple task would be made that much harder for me. I couldn't just nip to get what I'd forgotten; I couldn't do anything fast as once I would have been able to. I had learned to accept this, and instead I focused on all the positives in my life. By now a very long and ever growing list had formed.

As incredible as being a Mummy was, I knew that very soon I would need to do other things as well. I wouldn't always be able to spend the whole day just staring in wonderment at Maisie, admiring her and feeling pure contentment.

Soon I was back in the office doing a few hours a week. My Auntie Kerry looked after Maisie. The break and change of routine did me a lot of good, but then I would so look forward to collecting Maisie on my way home.

I'd become aware of my left leg having a lot of spasms, even lifting off the footplate of my chair. I knew this was an indication that something was wrong but I could not think what it could be. If I'd been skiing, or had fallen out of the chair recently, I might have thought it was a fracture, but neither was applicable. I was aware that it was fairly common for spinal injured patients to suffer fractures, due to osteoporosis. There was no swelling or bruising, and I'd done nothing untoward, so I ignored it. Maybe I just needed to exercise it more.

The spasms continued until a few weeks later, during the course of only one day, the leg became really badly swollen; my skin was so stretched that it appeared shiny. I showed it to Mum and we both feared it could be a blood clot, knowing that I was at a higher risk of having one because of my spinal injury and having been pregnant. For the duration of my pregnancy I had regular injections to thin my blood. I'd stopped having these about 4 weeks earlier thinking I would be fine now.

By now, it was early evening so I rang NHS direct and after loads of questions they told me I should go to the Walk-In Centre in Loughborough. Dan was still working in Southampton during the week so this time I left my Dad to look after Maisie, first giving him a quick lesson on how to change a nappy.

Mum and I headed off to Loughborough, which was a thirty minute car journey. The doctor there saw me but he sent me straight to Leicester Royal A&E, another decent drive. I asked him if I could go back home and then see someone first thing the following morning. "No," came his reply, "It is an emergency." It was a very long night; it was 3 a.m. when eventually I saw a doctor. It was very clear that he knew absolutely nothing about spinal injuries as, when he touched my leg causing a spasm, he nearly shot out the room. "Oh, I wasn't expecting that," he laughed. He couldn't believe that a paralysed leg moved. I was injected with a blood thinner, and would continue to this until I had the next appointment.

A couple of days later I was back for the appointment. The first thing the nurse said to me was, "You need to stand on the scales," and she followed this with, "Can you walk?" I was astonished. When I replied "No," she looked clearly shocked. The next question was no better, "Can you stand?" she asked. "No," I responded. "Ohhhh," came the bewildered response, she obviously could not believe it. Having just been through all of this, it was only minutes later when she told me that I must stand on the scales as she needed to weigh me. "I am paralysed," I said looking straight into her eyes and, then, pointing to my chest I continued, "Nothing works from here down, I CANNOT stand on the scales to be weighed."

I was exasperated. Honestly, this sort of thing almost drove me mad sometimes. I remember going to see my GP because I thought I had a urine infection and I was concerned I had kidney stones. He asked me if it stung when I went to the loo. I explained I had no sensation. Obviously, having totally ignored my response, he went on to tell me if I had kidney stones I would have low-backache. Why could I not get used to the fact that there was no understanding of the basic facts of a spinal cord injury?

Although my leg looked ready to burst, they were too busy to fit me in for a scan, so I was given another appointment for a fortnight later. In the meantime I had a busy few days, including a visit to Belton Horse Trials on the quad bike, with Maisie in a baby sling around my neck.

I returned to the hospital for my appointment and for the scan. They could not find the top of the clot but knew that it was close to my lungs. It was very serious, and as such, I was not even allowed to wander down the corridor to the hospital's Costa for a coffee, in case I dropped dead. After them allowing me to do whatever I wanted for the last two weeks, I found this absolutely unbelievable. They wanted me to stay there overnight but I had lost all confidence in their patient care, so I insisted on going home. I was on warfarin for a long time and had to have my IRN levels regularly checked; this measures how fast your blood clots, so the warfarin dosage can be adjusted accordingly. Although, over time the swelling reduced, my left leg remains slightly larger.

I had not forgotten about the Rewalk suit that I saw whilst I was planning my wedding. I had been in touch with them and it was going to be demonstrated at a mobility show at Birmingham NEC. The suit was made in Israel, and invented by a quadriplegic named Amit Goffer. He'd spent years working on this suit, and was now working on another suit that he would use in the future. He was certainly a man who had not let his horrific car accident stop him from getting on with his life.

This demonstration was an exhilarating opportunity to actually see the suit, so naturally we planned a trip there. I had already started to think that if I could get the suit and use it to walk the London Marathon, I might be able to raise some more money for Spinal Research. This prospect really stimulated me and I was desperately hoping I was not going to be disappointed when I saw the suit being used.

I was far from disappointed. In fact, I was immensely impressed when I saw a paraplegic walking independently around the NEC in the suit; he made it look easy. The price tag was £43,000; I needed to raise this to stand any chance of fulfilling my Marathon dream. I still had around £25,000 from various fundraising events so needed about another £20,000 to make this happen. I had hoped to get a hydrotherapy pool, but I decided that the money raised would now go towards this robotic suit.

When I told them my intention was to get one and to walk the marathon, they just went along with my idea. They did not really believe me, but they didn't know me. I returned home fired up, I was now a girl on a mission. The first job was to raise the money. Simple, another riders' naked calendar. This time I would ask riders not only from eventing, but showjumping and racing too. I told them my intentions were to go on and raise lots more money for Spinal Research. Once again their support was nothing short of amazing. With the help of my friends we planned some fantastic scenes. It all took off and with the support of so many kind people a 2012 calendar was produced.

Optimistic Matt Hampson could see my challenge being a huge success. He obviously believed in me. Matt had set up the Matt Hampson Foundation, a charity that helps injured sportsmen and women. He continued to fundraise and gave donations to people to get equipment, chairs, or whatever they needed. He also offered his support, and I already knew from my own experience how much he could help. Matt gave me a generous donation towards the suit. It was looking more and more likely that the amount I needed was achievable.

All London Marathon runners get their place a long time before the actual race day. I did not want to miss out. I spoke to the team at Spinal Research and secured my place for the 2012 Virgin London Marathon. Shortly after, I received my information pack and running vest, only to have one problem - the suit still wasn't available in the UK and I wouldn't be able to walk without it. Was it just a distant dream?

For the first time in four years I really enjoyed being back at
the Burghley Horse Trials. I was interviewed on the 'Celebrity Talk' stand, and afterwards I sold the calendars. It was a great launch for the calendar and I took about £3000 home at the end of the three days. I was again aware of how Maisie had totally changed my life. Bob was competing, but my pain was now minimal.

I had my little girl, no longer did I miss eventing or the horses. Thankfully, the days of watching the other riders compete and feeling my stomach churning with envy had passed. It was indeed a revelation when I realised that I would not turn the clock back to before my accident for anything; I could not imagine life now without Maisie and Dan.

I religiously stuck with my sessions on the treadmill, standing, FES bike and weekly physiotherapy with Kate; the thought of the marathon was keeping me motivated. I had somehow managed to rebuild my life. It was very different from my old life but there was one thing that both of them had in common, they were very busy. The only thing I felt I lacked was a summer sport.

I decided to give water skiing a go. Mum had Maisie for the day so that Dan and I could go off to give it a try. I had water-skied in Australia and I'd loved it. Today it was a session with the British Disabled Water Ski Association, as they had both the instructor and adaptive equipment. I hadn't given much thought to the fact that I wasn't over-confident in water, for the reason that I would be wearing a life jacket. That would be fine, or so I thought. We had to wait around for quite some time, but eventually it was my turn. I didn't find it anywhere near as difficult as snow skiing, but I found falling more unpleasant. It didn't hurt as much as a fall when snow skiing, but I panicked and almost drowned; well it felt as if I did. I went to use my legs to stop me sinking and that is when I became frightened. I felt hopeless. Somehow I managed to calm myself down and I started to float.

Even without this scary experience, water skiing didn't give me either the same buzz or the same freedom as did snow skiing. To water ski, I had to be towed by a boat and so was reliant on other people, whereas when I was monoskiing on the mountain I was on my own, doing my own thing. It had been worth the try but to be perfectly honest, it was a relief to finish; it was not for me.

I couldn't help but cringe when one of the instructors said: "Can your carer get you out of the boat please?" It was only a small thing but I didn't like it. That is why I so enjoyed going skiing with my friends and family; it is that indefinable joy, that feeling of being together and normality. Dan is my husband, he is not my carer, and I didn't like people presuming he was there to look after me.

These sporting groups are fantastic centres for many, but they just were not for me. I like to do sports with my old friends and family, and not be separated and grouped with other wheelchair users. I had felt like this since the early days after my accident, and I am not alone. I have met others who feel exactly the same. I've made friends with several spinal injured people, but this has not lessened the antipathy I have for being included in the category for 'disabled people'. I felt the same when I was pregnant.

I recall going on a ski holiday when, at the airport, there was a guy in a wheelchair and we got the lift onto the plane together. He was a monoskier too. He clearly hated others in wheelchairs too, because when I tried to chat to him he wouldn't even say hello. I had to smile to myself. Everyone reacts differently to an injury that comes with no warning. I wasn't quite like him. I just enjoyed doing my sports with my own friends. They made me feel as if life had not changed as dramatically as it would have felt, had I been surrounded only by wheelchair users.

That I had not enjoyed water skiing and that had been a real disappointment because I had pinned my hopes on it being my summer sport. I would have to continue the search because I still needed a sport to occupy me outside of the skiing season. For a couple of days I felt a bit flat, perhaps it was shock from almost drowning, but then I got an email about the suit. Great: just the distraction I needed.

I was invited to go to the Royal Bucks Hospital to see the suit again, and encourage this private hospital to buy it. The suit needed to be purchased by a rehabilitation centre in the UK where my training would take place.

Kate, Mum, Maisie, Rachel, and I all went to explore and to establish if this looked possible. I told them about my London Marathon place and showed them how enthusiastic I was. The hospital had to work out if it was worth the expense, and if they could make it a part of a business plan. The cost of the rehab suit was a staggering £100,000, so they would need to get plenty of users through the door to justify the expense. This suit was more than double the price of the one I'd seen earlier, because this was an adjustable version; it could be altered to fit anyone.

I didn't leave with the positive feeling that I had been hoping for. For a fleeting moment or two, I almost decided to stop dreaming about the marathon. We were getting ever closer to the race day, and things did not look very promising. There was a suit in a rehab centre in Italy. I enquired about that but it wasn't an option to go there.

I knew there was nothing more I could do. If ReWalk couldn't find a way to make this happen I certainly couldn't do any more. I had raised the money, I'd entered the marathon and I'd kept on at them to show my commitment, but none of this was working. I felt utterly deflated.

Another challenge I'd already embarked on was my own business: 'Dalliance'. I had been making use of the jewellery classes I'd attended with Sue, whilst I was expecting Maisie. I loved designing and making the jewellery. I'd set up my own website; I'd designed the webpage and decided the pricing, Dan had taken the photos. I'd tried to think of what would be the best ways to sell the jewellery. I knew about various discount webpages such as 'Groupon' and 'KGB Deals' so I contacted both. I heard back from KGB Deals, and sent them some of my jewellery to view. I secured a deal with some pearl earrings, the only piece of jewellery I could afford to put on at a significantly reduced price, and still make a little bit of money. They were quick to make and I bought the pearls in bulk, so they were cheaper. I was very excited to make £3000 profit from the deal. I was sick of the sight of the small fiddly parts, and the superglue. However, as intended, it got people visiting my website and some bought more jewellery. It was fun as I had never done anything like it, and I learned a lot. The lead up to Christmas was absolutely manic and I sold more than I ever expected. In order to start the business I'd spent a lot on buying stock of different pearls, beads, silver etc., but I was quite chuffed when I made a profit in my first year.

I was sitting comfortably on the floor, making a large order that I'd just received, and Maisie was sitting up, playing with her toys, when I received an email. It was the most exciting email, and a bit of a surprise. With a mixture of disappointment and reluctance I'd almost given up on the idea of the 2012 marathon. The email was from a UK clinic based near Hull; it had purchased the rehab version of the suit. I could hardly believe it, I was so thrilled, and my training could start as soon as it arrived.

I was going to be the first user in the UK, and the first person in the world to walk a Marathon in it. It was due to arrive in mid January. It was a real coincidence that Rachel, who had been involved in much of the fundraising, only lived 3 miles away from this clinic. She offered us a room whenever we needed it. I couldn't believe my luck. This would save so much money and make the few weeks more fun staying with a character like Rachel. But it would also mean that I had only 12 weeks in which to train for the London Marathon. Should I defer my entry for a year? Not a chance! I was going to do whatever it would take. It was December now and I was committed to two ski holidays before my challenge began.

We'd been skiing on the first week of the season for the past three years, and I was as keen as ever. However I did wonder how much skiing I would be able to do in future. I'd done nearly three years with Simply Morzine, and I now had Maisie. It was probably time to find new things to do; this is why I'd started my jewellery business. Once I'd completed the marathon, I would be able to invest more time into that over the summer and have things ready to sell pre-Christmas.

On this holiday not all the ski lifts were open in Morzine, so we went up to Avoriaz which is a higher resort. We got some truly fantastic skiing. I had two nannies for Maisie, and as it was a quiet week they worked in pairs. They were fantastic with Maisie, and she was very happy to be left with them each morning when we went off to ski. There were twelve of us so we filled the chalet.

What a difference the year had made. I had some great friends on this holiday, including Rachel, and we all had kids. It was very different to the trip the previous season, when there'd been no children except Maisie, and she was still in my tummy.

Mum, Dad and Sue were also with us. I was the lucky owner of a new monoski, a much better one. The previous season there had been a fire in the boot room at one of Simply Morzine's chalets and I had left my ski there. Gareth rang me to break the news thinking I would be a bit sad. I had rushed out to buy my first one, and now I would have the opportunity to buy a better one once I received the insurance money. With Dom's help I chose a new Praschberger monoski. I had one go indoors before the holiday to set it up and get used to it. This was my first ski holiday actually using it. The improvement in my skiing was incredible. I felt so much more in control, and the turns were easy.

On this particular day, I had just pulled over to the side of the piste to wait for the group. It was a fantastic feeling to have to be the one waiting for the others. It didn't seem long ago when everyone had to wait for me, or to pick me up. This wasn't the case anymore. The next thing I felt was an immense pounding in my side. I was in agony. A girl had crashed into me at speed. My initial thought was that I had broken my arm and the marathon dream was over.

I was annoyed to start with because the girl clearly wasn't safe to be on the piste alone, but she was apologetic and in a state of shock herself. She had apparently already taken her skis off and walked down some of the mountain, but had just put them back on when she lost control and whacked into me. Her friends had left her and she could have been seriously injured.

This happens too often in skiing, people do not think they need lessons, or they rely on their friends to try to teach them. My arm was black and severely sore that evening, but we were lucky not to have a more serious injury. Phew, the marathon dreams were still alive.

I managed to ski for the rest of the week and we'd had another super holiday. Getting back to see Maisie after skiing was the highlight of the day. The nannies took her out every day, and we were shown lots of photos in the evening. It was obvious she'd had some great days and had not missed us. Maisie was tucked up in bed by 7 o'clock and we could sit by the log fire with a drink followed by a delicious meal. This is a treat at the best of times but after a day skiing in the cold it was greatly appreciated.

I had only a couple of weeks at home before I went back out again for four days' skiing with my friend Helen, whom I had bought a horse from six months before my accident. We were now great friends. The one and only Henry also joined us. Mum looked after Maisie as Dan was working. We were lucky to have perfect snow and weather, something you have no control over but which makes a massive difference to the skiing. Poor conditions could make an easy slope difficult.

On this holiday the pistes were perfect, no ice, fresh snow and sunshine, of which Dan was very envious. He was at work whilst I was having the most awesome skiing. We went up to a webcam located at the top of one of the chairlifts we often used and told him to look. We waved frantically; I was easy to spot with fluorescent pink ski trousers and a pink mohican on my helmet.

I skied mainly with Henry. Helen was with her friend who was at a similar level and had also joined us on our trip. The new monoski was operating really well. I felt like a truly competent skier now. I enjoyed overtaking able-bodied people; this gave me a real buzz. This was definitely removing the 'dis' from disability. I had the ability to ski well, whereas when I put Henry in my ski, or Dan, they had the 'disability'. This sport had given me so much back of what I lost on that horrific day, and like eventing, it had given me the feeling of speed and the release of much needed adrenaline.

I could now confidently ski all the red runs. These are intermediate level slopes and they are all fairly difficult. Black runs are the equivalent to Advanced level eventing. I wanted to achieve this level; maybe there was a chance it could be on this holiday with these perfect skiing conditions?

Henry and I had just got on the chair-lift; I actually found that really nerve wracking. I had a few tumbles when we got the timing wrong. We were on safely and looking down at a black run, debating whether I should attempt it. At the top of the chair-lift I could either ski off to the left for the black run or to the right for a red run. I couldn't decide which at first but when I got to the top I skied off to the left.

I must have wanted to frighten myself to death. I skied down the gentle slope that took me to the top of the run. "Shit Henry, it looks steep. I want to go back," I said in a shaky voice. "Babes, I am not pushing you back up the hill, sorry," he said, with a look that meant it, but also a smirk as he too had seen the gradient of this daunting piste. I felt the same nerves as I did in the start box at Burghley. I was committed to it now; there was no going back according to Henry.

I skied off. 'Tight turns Claire, keep it steady,' I thought. If I kept the turns tight I wouldn't pick up too much speed, but on a slope like this if I ended up pointing my ski down the mountain for any length of time I would end up going like a bat out of hell. I lost it on one of the turns and fell. When the gradient is this steep I didn't just stop like I normally would, I travelled a fair way at quite a speed. Henry lifted me up and I managed to ski the rest perfectly well. I was damned chuffed. I had made my first black run with just one fall.

"Come on Henry, let's do it again." I'd had another moment of madness, so up the chair lift we went and once again turned left. At least I knew the run this time. I was still buzzing from the last run. I was getting each turn right and almost enjoying it. But then I left one turn a little late and went off the piste hitting a bump. It flung me up into the sky and as I came down my helmet and goggles came off along with my ski, which should never come off. My ski had a strong binding on designed specifically to stop it coming off in a fall, but this impact had caused it to detach itself from my bucket seat.

I somersaulted several times down the slope, terrifying myself in the process. It felt like an eternity, each time I flipped over I hoped I would stop. Eventually I did. I took a deep breath, opened my eyes and lay there very still. I was fine but it had been extremely scary and, what was even more frightening was, I still had a very long way to ski. I was absolutely petrified but Henry was even more so. He skied over, and looking ashen he peered over me, "You could have bloody waved your arms, I thought you had broken your effing neck this time."

We sat on the piste for a while to recover from the shock. It took a few minutes before we managed to laugh about it, but later we relived the black run when we told Helen all about our escapades. I'd learned a few lessons. One being I must do up my chinstrap more tightly; my hat flying off was not something I wanted ever to experience again.

It was a relief when I skied the rest of the slope well. I was thrilled to be able to say that I had achieved a black run, but for the moment I was happy to stay on the reds. I was a Mum and I had responsibilities.

That night I had flashbacks to the fall, but Henry was fast asleep and snoring. It couldn't have worried him too much even though he went on to tell everyone about my acrobatics on the black run. I'd skied it well, and the tumble didn't make me lose confidence. I had misjudged the edge of the piste and was unfortunate to hit a bump, a bit like I was unfortunate to hit a tree! However, I did feel as if, perhaps, I should take it a bit easier now.

I returned from the holiday and had the weekend in which to recover before my first day's training commenced for the 2012 London Marathon. I had been waiting for this day; I was prepared. I was used to being upright from all the treadmill work, and standing in the frame, but this would be different. I didn't know what to expect. What would it feel like? Would it be difficult? How much training would I need? All these questions would soon be answered.

8

Undoubtedly, what I was about to embark upon was going to have to be an enormous commitment for the next few months. The car was rammed full with everything we should need, including Maisie's walker and toys to keep her occupied whilst I was training. The journey took two and a half hours; my training was 20 miles east of Hull.

Mum and I chattered non-stop, both of us very excited to see how I would get on with walking in the suit. It seemed as though I had been chasing this dream for a very long time now.

Eventually we arrived at the village hall, close to the rehab clinic that was in the final stages of being built. I had met the owners of the business when I was at the NEC and at the Royal Bucks Hospital. Inside the village hall there was a gathering of people for me to meet. There was a physiotherapist from the UK, another from Israel and one from the ReWalk team. There were also three other staff from the Cyclone team: Ian, Les and Sarah.

The entire morning was spent setting up the adjustable suit to fit me. All my measurements were taken and passed over to Ian who was responsible for putting the suit all together. I was eager to get in the suit but it was essential that it fitted perfectly. There was quite a buzz in the room. Cyclone were excited to see the first person in their suit. With support from hundreds of people, I had worked hard to make this happen. I felt sure that my continuous rehab could only be a benefit; I was fit and well and ready to learn to walk. If I'd done what I'd been told to do and had not been on my feet for the five years, then it could have been a very different story. It might even have been dangerous to suddenly stand up.

FES cycling and standing had helped my bone density stay as strong as possible and, hopefully, had alleviated the danger of osteoporosis, another complication of spinal injuries. The physiotherapist checked my range of movement and I did some leg stretches, all in preparation for my first session in the suit. I would be the first person in the country to even stand in the suit.

The suit was sat on a wide chair and I was lifted into it. There it was in all its glory; this gleaming exoskeleton was going to enable me to walk again. The suit was heavy with plastic strips down the sides of my legs; these had joints at the knee and hip. It had metal posts that ran along the side of my body and a rucksack containing the battery and computer. Straps were pulled very tight to secure my legs in place. There was a 'wrist watch' that operated the different modes or functions the suit was able to perform. The physio worked this for now so I could focus on the standing up and walking.

'Beep, beep, beep,' was the sound before I was given a firm push to stand upright. Eventually I would be responsible for doing all this, but to start with I needed assistance.

Everyone looked at my face to see my reaction to being upright, wondering if it would be an emotional experience, now I was standing tall. It would be easy to understand if I shed a few tears, but it didn't feel at all strange to me because of all the work I had done since my accident, I was used to standing up. However, what did feel different was how tall I felt. In my standing frame my knees were slightly flexed, as my pelvis leans back on the strap, but the biggest difference was I had no support around me. When I was in the wooden standing frame, there was a table attached where my laptop usually sat, the treadmill had a control panel directly in front of me. Now there was nothing.

"I forgot how small you were," I cheekily said to Mum. I had spent five years looking up at people. Now, standing, I could talk to people on an eye-to-eye level or in some cases look down at them. This was fantastic; it made me feel so good about myself.

The first stage was to improve my standing balance. To me there was no floor, I couldn't feel a thing. I felt like I was floating. I glanced down at my feet, they were definitely there, ready to go. I had only been standing up for a few minutes and my hands started to hurt. They were bright red and throbbing from the pressure being applied to them. I needed to adjust my balance so my legs took all my weight, not my arms that were presently gripping tightly on to the crutches with much of my weight pushing through them.

I was surrounded by three people, so should I lose my balance I wouldn't fall. I was safe and I needed to be brave. But how was I ever going to trust my legs to support me when I couldn't feel they were there? It was training my brain as much as anything. The trouble was, because my arms were out in front of me I felt unlikely to topple forwards, but if I stood totally upright I might over adjust and I had nothing that would stop me from falling backwards. I spent some time just moving my crutches to the side, in front and behind me. When I was leaning forward on them too much, not only did the pain I felt in my hands and wrists nearly kill me, but the crutches felt like they were being sucked deep into the ground. Lifting them was near to impossible.

There was nobody in the room who'd had much experience with the system. In fact, it was such new, pioneering equipment that we were all learning together.

145

After a lunch break, it was my first attempt at a few steps. I was focused, I meant business, and I was full of determination.

The control watch had a 'walk mode' button, which the physio pressed. One beep was given and I would start walking; except I didn't. Nothing happened at all. I had Ian on one side and Les on the other, with their hands firmly holding on to the side of the suit. The physio was standing in front to offer some advice, but she was no more clued up on the suit than I was. The physio from Israel had some experience and tried to explain.

"The right leg always takes the first step. There is a sensor above your pelvis; you have to shift your weight onto your left leg when you hear the beep. This will enable the right leg to lift up and take a step forwards. Let's try again."

'Beep,' I thought I had put my weight on the left leg; still nothing happened. "Bugger," I said. "I thought I'd shifted my weight, but obviously I didn't."

This happened a few times and I was starting to feel confused. What the hell was I supposed to do? I wasn't offered any more advice; it had to be a case of trial and error. Les was holding the suit on the right side so, as the watch was pressed and the beep was heard, he literally lifted that side up to free the weight off my right leg, and a step was taken. One step. Well, it was a start! We all cheered.

Eventually we managed to get a few steps strung together but it was basically using Ian's and Les's strength to lift each side. I concentrated on my balance and just trying to get the feel of what I should do, but this was still knackering. "Maybe Ian and Les should have a marathon place too, I may need them," I joked.

We had only a five minute drive to Rachel's large farm house. Rachel was a great friend to spend an evening with after a frustrating day of trying to master walking, a task that most people do every day without even thinking. She cooked us a delicious dinner and her lively, colourful, fun conversations were the remedy I needed to set me up for another session in the village hall.

Rachel had turned a lounge into a downstairs bedroom. Maisie had a cot next to me. Mum slept in a room upstairs.

The routine on the second day was much the same as the first. I managed to walk the length of the village hall a few times, and did a few more consecutive steps than I did the previous day. Les and Ian gradually did less but were there to correct my balance if I got it wrong. I had to get both the timing of the tilt and how much tilt exactly right, and the only way I stood a chance of achieving this was by staring down at my feet. This would cause me to lean forward obviously, and to put more strain through my wrists and hands. I tried to do it by looking forwards but I didn't have a clue where my legs were; I wouldn't even know which leg was taking the step.

There was certainly plenty for me to think about after these two days. I spent time watching a video of the Israeli guy walking in the suit. He made it look easy; why was I finding it so difficult?

He had been using the suit a long time now, so maybe he went through a similar learning process. I visualized myself walking well, getting the tilt right and was eager for my next two days. We had decided four hours training in a day was ample, so I did an afternoon training and then went back for a second session the next morning.

I spent the rest of the week working areas of my rehab that could possibly improve my walking, such as strengthening my core. There were flickers of muscle activity but it was still very weak and floppy, making even standing tall for a long period of time seem like hard work.

The next time, I did improve. I wasn't as good as I had hoped to be, but as long as I did better than the previous session, then I was moving in the right direction. It was the first couple of steps that I was struggling to get unless Les and Ian lifted the side of the suit but then, after about three steps, I could usually manage a few without their assistance.

I was learning so much about the technology. If I didn't tilt my pelvis enough, my leg taking the step would catch on the floor and the suit would stop. If I overdid the tilt, my leg taking the step would clang into the other leg, also causing me to come to a grinding halt.

Up and down the village hall I would go. I was putting every ounce of effort I could muster into this. I knew I had set myself a ridiculous goal but I was determined to achieve it. It had taken me almost five minutes to walk the length of the village hall.

"Eleven weeks to go, 26.2 miles to walk." We all laughed, sat down and had a rest.

Up I got for another attempt. I pressed the button on the watch, waited for the third beep, a big push on my crutches, which I was holding out to the side and slightly behind, and I was up. At least I could do that on my own now. My walking was better this time, maybe I was starting to crack it. The wall of the room was getting closer, very close, too close. "How do I bloody stop?" I yelled. I felt like I was in the 'wrong trousers' from Wallace and Gromit. I had been so desperate to get moving that I hadn't considered stopping, it simply hadn't entered my head. Les dived in to help and I did

148

stop. "Damn it, I really thought for a minute that I was going to walk up the wall," I said with a wide grin. I had made progress!

Over the two days I started to do more consecutive steps but I still needed to learn how to do the first one independently and, of course, stopping would be useful as well. That was the aim of the next session.

I think Maisie wondered what I was doing. She spent much of her time trying to wipe me out as she buzzed around in her walker. We were both finding our feet. Who would be walking first? She looked up at me, and I could see her thinking, 'Mummy is tall really'.

Ten weeks to become good enough to start the marathon was not very long but I knew I would be there no matter what it took. There was of course the occasional doubt in my mind, usually when I was in the suit. Having my positive family and many friends surrounding me, supporting me, believing in me was invaluable; soon the negativity vanished.

I constantly thought back to the early skiing lessons. I was convinced then that there could not have been a worse skier but now I was a competent skier. I had even taken on a black run. I told myself: 'The accomplishments that are the toughest give you the most satisfaction when you achieve them.' It would be boring if the marathon was easy. What would be the sense of achievement if I was strolling around with ease? Typically, as was my style, I was going to give this my all.

Exploring the media side was the next thing on my agenda. Since my accident I'd had regular local coverage from the TV and papers, but this was a whole new ball game. Media agencies had approached me after seeing a piece in the Leicester Mercury about my marathon dream. They wanted to do all my media and press work but it would be exclusive to them and would mean me losing control.

The decision was made not to use an agency, partly because Dave, from Cyclone, wanted to use his own PR and didn't agree with going along the agency route. That meant that I was going to be left to manage all the press as well as training hard for the actual challenge.

All the people in the equestrian world who had raised the money for me to eventually get the suit, of which £23,000 had already been paid, deserved to know how I was getting on. A Horse and Hound journalist rang me and put an article online about my early training sessions. On my next visit to the clinic I was waiting to start, and Mum had nipped to the car with Maisie to get her toys. As soon as she left the room Dave expressed how unhappy he was with the video link being shown. It was simply me learning to walk again and, in my opinion, there was nothing wrong with the video. Admittedly I was not marching along but that was the reality of it. All it did was generate interest in my challenge and his business. I was upset that he was so angry, and that day changed things for me. I didn't look forward to going to Hull for my sessions.

The rest of the staff were fantastic though and a new physio, Matt, soon joined the team. He had no experience of the suit but was a quick learner and his young 'go get em' attitude was ideal for what I had ahead of me. Matt was brave at trying new methods of learning and experimenting; it was brilliant to have him to work with. Soon I was able to have sessions just with Matt. He would walk behind me and, if at any time we needed more help, Les or Ian would be nearby.

We were in the completed clinic now and had more space to walk. I worked on turns as well as straight lines and I now had control of the watch that sent a wireless signal to the computer in the rucksack. Sometimes my hands would be burning hot and when I took my gel gloves off they were glowing. My wrists were excruciatingly painful but it was something I would have to endure because I wanted this so badly, I was desperate to walk across that finish line.

Kate also came to watch my training and although more opinions were great, it basically came down to practice. A lot of the time I knew what I was doing wrong but because I was physically challenged, I couldn't always control the precise movement.

It was repetition that I needed and I began to do circuits around the room. It was far from easy but I was getting better. I was still a long way off walking a marathon though. Thoughts would run through my head, '26.2 frigging miles at this pace.' I would also drive along in my car and clock how far a mile was. Some days I thought it was achievable; on others I thought I was mental, depending on my frame of mind.

Our evenings with Rachel always made us laugh; she thought I might need a bus time-table for the London Marathon, after watching a training session. I hadn't even tried to walk outside yet.

My marathon dream was starting to generate media interest. I had emailed ITV's 'Daybreak' and shortly after got a phone call from them arranging a time to film me in the suit, as well as a morning when I'd go in to the studio. By now I was frequently being filmed. Both my local news stations were coming, 'Inside Out' for East Midlands and now 'Daybreak'.

I ventured outside in the suit. My heart sank. It was even more difficult than I could have anticipated; every slope and every bump was a mountain. My foot would catch the ground as it stepped through and I would have to restart the suit only to get the tilt wrong again. It was a nightmare.

The smooth surface of the clinic was much easier; outside I had to increase the tilt so that my foot could clear the uneven ground. I was going to have to spend a lot of time outside over the next few weeks trying to master this. Just as I thought I was walking better I felt like it was day three all over again. I looked at my watch, half an hour had passed by and I had moved fifty pathetic yards. I rolled my eyes in despair.

"Bloody hell, what am I doing wrong? What is wrong with me?" I said, as I looked over at Matt and Mum. They could see I was frustrated, Mum recognized this face from the days I fell and fell whilst learning to ski. If it had not been for the marathon I might have given up, but I had launched into it wholeheartedly which helped me to stick at it when it was tough. I reminded myself, 'Failing is not an option'.

Dan and I had been into the make-up room and we were all ready for our first interview. We were in the green room waiting to be called through to the studio. I was concerned about Dan being on the show. He is quiet at the best of times so I was worried how he would deal with it, knowing that there were thousands of people watching him, but Daybreak were really keen to have Dan and Maisie on the sofa too. Dan and I were shaking with nerves. I looked at Dan and he was a shade of green, he was really terrified. Maisie though was loving it; aged only 1 and her first TV appearance.

There was one step up to the sofa so Dan lifted me up and put me on the sofa. He positioned himself next to me. We had a quick chat to the presenters, Dan Lobb and Helen Fospero, during the adverts, and this put us at ease. As soon as transmission started my nerves went and Dan spoke really well and confidently, but it was Maisie who stole the show. At the end of the interview I asked if I could ask them a question instead. Dan and Helen looked a little anxious.

"I am trying to get celebs to join me for a short part of my marathon and wondered if you could walk with me at any point?" To my utter delight, both of them agreed, and Dan said he was going to start training. I absolutely loved my first live interview; it left me wanting to do more. The whole studio had a warm, friendly atmosphere and the presenters were brilliant.

Once I'd been seen on one TV show, or in a newspaper article, it led to many more. It wasn't long before I was invited on to 'Live with Gabby' on Channel 5. I saw how much Dan had enjoyed Daybreak and he was also keen to do it again. This was just the start to what was going to be a crazy few months of media. I knew it was going to be a mixture of joy and exhaustion but, if I was going to raise anywhere near my ambitious target of £50,000, I needed to put some effort into this too.

My initial target was actually £10,000 but I decided to be brave and increase it to £50,000 because I didn't want people to stop donating because they thought I'd reached my goal. The revised target was ambitious and if I achieved it I would be amazed.

The media side was fantastic, so enjoyable but I knew, even without reminding myself, that if I fell short of putting enough effort into the serious training, I would struggle to do the marathon. I had to try to balance everything I was doing; all the training, the media, and being a mum. At times I was exhausted. Training days passed; there was a mixture of good and bad sessions. How could I walk well one day and so badly on others? Sometimes it just went like that. I persevered and I earnestly believed that I would do it, but when I was on the TV and heard myself saying I was walking the marathon, it did feel as if it was all a joke, unreal. Up to

153

that point, the furthest distance I had walked was no more than a quarter of a mile.

Matt had helped me so much and now I was walking down the road without being held at all. He was as ambitious for me as I was. The sore arms and hands refused to go away, but I was walking with an improved posture and my confidence was growing all the time. That was until I saw a pot-hole at the side of the road coming up, and the distraction of where to put my crutch, the hesitation and uncertainty, caused me to go flying. Although Matt slowed the fall slightly by hooking his fingers around the pelvic bar, he couldn't save me. As I hit the ground, Dan stood there catching it on film. I landed right in the muddy puddle which actually made me laugh, and instantly I wanted to see the video. It was brilliant.

I was fine, but the concerns were with the suit. A thorough check showed that we had got away without any damage. Matt was shocked by the fall but relieved that everything was OK. After this fall I actually walked better, so it appeared it hadn't affected me or my confidence. However, I was now acutely aware of how easily I could lose it, making us all rethink. I was lucky to be injury free. After all this driving to Hull, sometimes twice a week, as we tried to fit in extra sessions, I would have been gutted if an injury had stopped me chasing my dream.

Matt walked behind me with his hands gently on the pelvic bar so if I lost my balance he could grab me. The marathon wasn't going to be on a smooth wooden floor and we were now on a mission to do as much road walking as possible.

It was only six weeks until the 22nd April; the all-important day was looming. It didn't take much to work out that this journey into the unknown was going to take a long time. I also knew that the cost of a hotel in London wouldn't be cheap but I had to have somewhere to stay. Initially I was rather hoping to have enough money from the media agency to pay for our accommodation but I was now on a steep learning curve searching for, and discovering, which magazines and papers actually paid for interviews.

I had an interview with a great guy, Richard, from the Sunday Telegraph. He and I got on well, and I explained my circumstances. The Telegraph wouldn't pay for an interview but I asked Richard to include something in the article about my request. He told me that his sister was employed in the hotel business and he would ask her. I had already emailed several hotels but didn't get a single reply, so I didn't get my hopes up.

I wrote on my Facebook page that I was getting closer to the start and that I needed somewhere to stay. Not long afterwards, I saw a message in my inbox. It was from a friend of a friend named Louenna. She lived in Kensington, and I simply couldn't believe what I was reading. Louenna generously offered to move in with a friend and let us use her basement flat for as long as it took me to walk the route. She included some photos and it was seriously smart. A small problem was the stairs down to it, but we would deal with this, even if it meant my going up and down them on my bum. It would be perfect for Maisie as well, because she could be put to bed and we could have our dinner after. Perfect.

It was only two days later when I received an email from Richard. His sister had found a hotel in which I could stay for the duration of the walk. Thanks to Louenna I was sorted now though. Nevertheless, I clicked on the link to see which hotel it was. There was silence as I saw the page; I was gob smacked. I was being offered a room in one of the smartest hotels in

London, Chancery Court. It was a stunning 5-star in High Holborn; there was no way I could turn this down. Mum, Dad, Sue, Dan and everyone else I showed it to had a similar reaction. Yes, I now had two places to stay but with different friends and family planning to come to join me, it could work out perfectly.

I was in London for the 'Live with Gabby' show when we had our first stay at Chancery Court. Astrid, the manager, gave us the warmest welcome. Maisie was even given the largest teddy bear I had ever seen; it was waiting for her in her cot. The hotel was every bit as posh as it looked on the website. Wow, this was unbelievable. Not only were we in a beautiful hotel but the staff were the friendliest team you could wish for. I had a signed Good Luck card from all of the staff; this journey I was on felt magical already.

I was so excited for the marathon to start. Almost everything was going to plan with the preparations, even though the actual walking was more than a struggle. I was always led to believe that I would have support from Cyclone to help me throughout the marathon. Dave then told me I needed to find my own help. I was rather panicked by this. When I then asked to borrow the suit for a weekend prior to the marathon in order for my team to become more experienced, I was not allowed. All these difficulties added to the stress of this huge challenge. I had loved seeing Rachel every week and I'd enjoyed working with the rest of the staff but now I was looking forward to my last day so I didn't have to attend the clinic any more.

We had squeezed in a Saturday training day so Dan was able to come. Matt showed him how the suit worked and we had a decent session. We slotted in an extra walk at the weekends if we could. The following week we set off with a mission. Dan and I met Matt there. I was purely there to cover the distance and I was not being given much feedback when I made mistakes. I managed a mile. It felt like the longest mile ever possible. Alternating, Matt and Dan walked behind me, and we had the Garmin on to measure the distance. I was 300 meters short of the mile when I approached the entrance back to the clinic. I had set my heart on achieving my target of a mile.

Matt and Dan both said if you want to leave it there then do, we are close to that mile. I forced every extra step, throbbing arms, sore hands and an aching brain but I was thrilled to have made it, and so was Matt. He must have wondered if I would manage this marathon, but he always remained positive.

We were also sorting out everything I would need. We had a very dry spring and hardly any rain so it hadn't stopped me walking. The suit was not waterproof and it was unlikely that it would be dry every day whilst I walked the 26 miles. Mum sorted the problem by buying some XXL waterproofs to go over the suit. I tried them on top of the suit, and everyone took the piss. I looked clinically obese with an arse double its size.

Another thing we had to consider was what I would do when I needed a rest, which looked at being fairly often. It was essential I sat down every 90 minutes to loosen the straps. I could not feel if any of the straps was pinching or if there were any rubs, so it was important we did our best to prevent both. Either could have put a stop to my marathon dream.

With the robotic suit on I could not fit in Percy. Dan and I went shopping to search for a wide stool. We found the perfect solution. It was both foldable and lightweight so it could be carried easily. It was made out of canvas so, to make it steadier for me to sit on, we put a piece of wood on top.

T-shirts had also been printed with my text code and the names of a few of my sponsors, including Chancery Court Hotel.

The lead up to my very special day had been stressful but finally everything was coming together. I had eventually been informed by Matt that he would be there on day one, which was fabulous news, as well as Ian and Les. It had gone from no-one to three of them. I also had Mum, Dad, Dan, Maisie and my good friend Bec all coming down. There were enough of us to will me to walk.

I had my last stay at Rachel's and we celebrated with a lovely dinner party. Rachel had helped me make this journey possible in so many ways, from fundraising to her 'everything is possible' mentality that got me through those days when I returned to her lovely farmhouse after training, feeling a bit disappointed. Even the toughest days trying to string together three or four steps, had ended with many laughs. I had got to know Rachel well and we became great friends. We loaded up the suit, which I had named Fred, into the car. Fred and I were about to start our big adventure.

The Saturday morning before the big day I had arranged a
quick visit to Tesco in my home town of Melton Mowbray. We had permission to collect for charity and it was a good last practice before the race started. Kate, Dan and Sue had all practised helping with Fred, getting very familiar with all the straps. I walked up and down the aisles. It certainly had not become natural yet. Each step required concentration and, if I was distracted at all, I would fail to get the tilt right and my foot would not get the clearance it needed to do a step. I did stand on a lady's toe; I had one of the moments when I

158

couldn't stop. Bless her, she forgave me and even donated.

I had not found the walking easy and other people who had used the suit in America and Israel did a better job than me. What I found immensely difficult was not having a clue where my legs were and also the lack of control over my core. In training I had found that when I became fatigued it was because my core had nothing left in it; I became very wobbly.

The training I did was different from what others would do. I had thrown myself into an immense challenge and because of the distance I had to cover after only 12 weeks, my training was not spent working on technique and balance for as long as it would normally have been. It was all about how far I could walk. I had put huge amounts of pressure on myself and I started to feel it at times, with lots of media contacting me followed by radio interviews, newspaper interviews, and magazine interviews. It had not been easy by any stretch of the imagination and it was impossible not to feel nervous about the journey ahead but mixed with the nerves and anticipation was tremendous excitement.

It must have been a world record for cramming so much into one car. There were numerous checks to make sure nothing had been forgotten. Dad was driving down later with Bec and his car was also full to the brim with all the things we needed. We decided we would all stay in Louenna's flat for our first night, as we could all be together. When we pulled up she was waiting for us with all her bags packed to move out. I had never met her before and was overwhelmed once again by how kind and trusting she was. We had a lovely evening meal and the flat was full. Mum and Dad in one room, Bec on the sofa, Matt on an airbed in the corridor, leaving Dan, Maisie and myself in the other room. I laid out my clothes, gel gloves, trainers and my number was ready to pin onto my top. Fred was checked a dozen times to make sure he was on charge along with the control watch. All of us were terrified at the thought of a flat battery.

I needed a good night's sleep ready for what would no doubt be a long, hard but exciting day ahead. It was not to be. Maisie had been poorly with a cold and was snoring all night. I couldn't sleep. I tried counting sheep. I tried visualising walking – left, right, left, right. I even tried shoving tissue in my ears. I was getting wound up knowing I needed the rest and I would be starting out tomorrow feeling tired but nothing seemed to work. Not ideal. I tossed and turned, I looked at my watch; the more I tried to sleep the more impossible it seemed. I was frustrated.

I heard some movement. Apparently Matt had a poor night too. He'd had nightmares about me falling, and he had woken up grabbing the edge of the bed as if it was me and Fred.

We were certainly fired up for this important day; the day I had spent so much time working towards. I eventually nodded off at 4:00 am. I dreamed I was walking the London Marathon and then I awoke to live the dream.

9

My stomach churned like a washing machine: this was my first competition since the day of my accident. I was about to undertake a personal challenge; if I could make it to the finish line days later in 37,500th position, otherwise known as last, then I would still be a winner. I would have achieved my goal.

I was staring out of the car window, looking at the London pavements; never before had I even noticed, never mind studied them intently for every incline, defect or roughness. "Ummm, this could be tricky, in fact next year's runners may overtake me," I said to Dan. "You will be fine," replied Dan with great confidence, knowing I needed the reassurance.

It was the day I had been working desperately hard for, the build-up had been stressful but finally the 22nd April 2012 was here. We were on our way to the start of the Virgin London Marathon.

As we got closer the roads were closed to traffic, but special allowances had been made for us. We felt like royalty; we had permission to park as close to the start as possible. I saw the three balloons high up in the sky showing the different starts. We were here, and with plenty of time to prepare. We began to unload: crutches, stool, Fred, waterproofs, padding for legs, collecting tins, t-shirts and maps. My nerves began to show when I had to check at least five times that we had everything, and nothing was going to be left behind. Dan and Matt picked up all the equipment and we headed into the area where the athletes were gathering. The sun was shining, and there was a real buzz as all the competitors got closer and closer to setting off on a challenge they had all worked so hard for, and had spent much of the winter training out in the cold. A high fence surrounded the entire area and there was very strict security at the entrance. Everything about this whole event felt like a very big deal and I was so proud to be one of the competitors. I had been allocated two extra passes for my helpers, so we showed these to the security men, entered the area and joined the rest of the athletes. Dan and Matt were absolutely essential to me. I needed one to walk behind me and the other to push Percy, my chair, which would be piled up with the stool and other equipment. It steadied my nerves knowing I had such a fantastic team in support.

By now, the atmosphere was electric and my excitement continued to grow. The green start was the 'celebrity area', so my eyes were peeled as I tried to spot some of the well-known runners, but I was distracted by some of the most incredible fancy dress outfits. One runner was dressed as the Eiffel Tower; he couldn't even fit under the starting banner as his costume was so tall. I wondered if there was anyone who thought I was in fancy dress as the 'Bionic Woman'.

Matt went to investigate where I was supposed to be. He returned shortly with all the information we needed. I was told to wait at the side of the barriers near to the start line and then, once the last of the runners had passed through, I could step out and begin my journey. I was relieved to hear they didn't expect me to walk from the back of the long line of competitors, as this would have meant that I would need a rest by the time I actually reached the start line. Every step was an effort so I certainly didn't want to do any extra.

Before we went into position I did a couple of interviews with my local TV news channels. I had got to know them a little now so it was great to see their familiar faces, along with local radio and an equestrian journalist.

"So how are you feeling Claire? Are you ready for this?" I was asked.

I was more than ready for it but I had found the last few weeks of training exceptionally difficult, and I was certainly not going to miss driving to Hull twice a week. I was also relieved I was here; I now knew it was possible I could achieve the whole distance. My excitement outweighed my nerves, I was eager to take that first step of a very long and steady journey.

Dan carried Fred, who was seated on the wide stool, over to the barrier where I was lifted into him. Then, the ten straps were done up tightly with plenty of protective padding in. It was essential we did all we could to prevent any sores; I would be mortified if I couldn't complete this marathon because of a sore. Just as I had fastened my control watch on I heard a friendly voice. It was Charlie, another runner raising money for the same charity - Spinal Research. He jogged over from his start to meet me. Both Charlie and I had mutual friends from the eventing world and had been in touch via Twitter throughout our training though we had never met until now. We wished each other heaps of luck, and Charlie promised he would come back to help for the rest of the marathon. He seemed very confident he would beat me, and he couldn't quite believe the challenge I had set myself.

I pressed the 'stand up' button, put my crutches behind me and pushed myself up. My legs spasmed and shook. They do this when I go from sitting to standing because the muscles feel the stretch; the sitting position shortens my hamstrings and calves. Another reason standing is so good for me.

Charlie jogged off to his starting area and I was now standing tall. That was better, I could see so much more, and I took in the views as I prepared myself for one of my most important days so far. Glancing around

I could see hundreds of fit athletes stretching, shaking their limbs and warming up. I just stood there saving all my energy, fixed firmly in to my robotic suit, with my gel gloves protecting my hands whilst I gripped the crutches. The runners lined up and were packed in tightly, all itching to set off. Near the front was Will Young with his headphones on looking very focused. Then the lovely Susanna Reid from BBC Breakfast came over to wish me luck. She said she would come back and join me at some point. I was taken aback by her kindness, as if she didn't have a totally manic lifestyle already with young children and work commitments, but she was clearly a lovely person and wanted to show her support.

The deafening horn was blown. They were off. I watched them as they placed one foot in front of the other. Could this upset me, seeing everyone run freely? I was soon going to be left behind; these runners would soon fade into the distance.

Every step for me was an effort not just physically but mentally too. I was going to have to concentrate every second of the way, but I was really hungry for this challenge. As the last of the runners crossed the start line the moment was here. The barrier was pulled open, Matt helped me get over to the start line and I was ready to go.

I pressed the walk button on my control watch, heard the beep and shifted my weight onto my left leg. Looking down I could see my right leg pick up and I took the very first step of what would be many thousands if I were to reach the finish line. The crowd cheered loudly. By now all the other competitors had disappeared into the distance and so I knew all this was for me; goose bumps rose on my arms. I felt proud to be walking, I didn't even wish I was running, this was immensely rewarding. My eyes welled up, but I was so buoyed up I found it easy to give one of my biggest smiles, even though I was in full concentration. People were calling my name, encouraging me and wishing me luck. I did some of my best ever steps and travelled at my quickest pace. I was worried how many times I would catch my foot and come to a standstill but by now I truly was on a mission. Matt was right behind me, and Dan at my side pushing Percy, my chair. The reaction of the crowd was unbelievable; none of us had expected it to be like this. It was a moment I shall never forget. Journalists showed a real interest in my challenge and camera men were snapping shots left right and centre. Was this really happening to me?

Only five years earlier I had kissed goodbye to experiencing such highs, I thought my life couldn't have moments as exciting as competing at events such as Burghley. It was a fact then that I thought my life was ruined forever.

Today was even more special than my eventing high. It all began with fighting away the darkest days which had drained me of more strength than had the hardest day training in the suit. Yes, it had taken me years to make it here. This wasn't simply the result of a 12-week training programme, this was the culmination of five years of perseverance, patience, persistence, hope and commitment, with countless tears, total frustration, and anger all thrown in.

The Virgin London Marathon was going to be a gruelling challenge, but possibly no harder than forcing myself to go on the treadmill each day, or the FES bike when no one was around and I was feeling low.

I was ready for a break so I stopped, leaned back on to Matt who took my weight, so my arms and hands could rest. They were burning already but a short rest relieved them. "Bloody hell, did you expect this reaction?" I said to Matt and Dan. I certainly hadn't. Radio 5 Live approached me for an interview. Dan and I both spoke about my marathon attempt, both overwhelmed by the crowd's reactions and trying our best to hold back the tears. It was seriously difficult as the emotions were flooding through my body. I felt grateful and revved up about this opportunity I had been given. Photos and filming continued, crowds cheered and generous donations were being thrown into Dan's collection bucket. We joined up on the same route as the competitors from the 'blue start'. Runners were passing me clapping and shouting words of support. This was mind blowing, I was getting serious encouragement and I knew this would stick with me for the quieter days that would surely lie ahead.

We continued on our way. My head was down, 'right tilt, left tilt, right tilt, left tilt', when out of the corner of my eye I saw a man running out of his shop towards us. He went straight over to Dan and emptied the contents of his till into the collection bucket, except much of it spilled onto the floor. Dan picked up all the money and added it to the quickly filling bucket. Such generosity left us all amazed and speechless. "Thanks so much," I managed to shout as I walked slowly on.

Mum, Dad, Bec and Maisie all caught up with us eventually. They had been on the busy Tube and it had taken them quite a while to get to us. It was a real shame they had missed the start because it was hard to explain exactly how breathtaking the experience had been. I am sure Mum would have been in tears. It was difficult not to be moved by so many people giving so much support. Les and Ian caught us up there too, along with a couple of friends including Kathryn, who was my midwife, and Hannah.

The walking continued. I wanted to get as far as I possibly could on day one because the roads were closed. This allowed me to walk in the centre of the road, which was easier as it was flatter than the pavements. I was impressed by how much ground we had covered.

We were ready for a short break and a bite to eat. I heard the news that the first woman had not long finished in an impressive time of two hours eighteen minutes. Whilst we had a break I was relieved to see my skin looking fine, there were no marks or sore areas to worry about. I would be stopping for lunch at just over a mile in. My aim for day one was at least two miles so it was a quick pee and drink in one of the only pubs we passed; they were not serving food. We all sat around outdoors having our lunch which was the best we could get, a pizza take-away. It was a chance to get out the suit and give my brain a rest as well as my aching body. There was a real feel good factor amongst us as the time arrived to walk again. It started to cloud over in the afternoon so we tested out the waterproofs. They were not easy to get on, and it took a team of us. Once I had them on I looked ridiculous but they did the job and that was the main thing, fashion didn't come into it. I kept on going, one foot in front of the other, and then the rain started to come down. I received a text message from Matthew Pinsent saying he would be arriving soon on his motorbike. By now I was exhausted and ready to pack up for the day, but the four-time Olympic gold medalist was joining me to walk after he had heard about my challenge, and there was not a chance I was going to look tired in front of him.

Matthew's presence made me walk further than I thought was ever possible, and having one of the greatest sports stars with me gave me that spurt of energy to walk the last quarter mile up a hill. I finished by chatting to Matthew, and it was a good job I was in Fred because even then he towered above me. Sitting down and chatting could have given me a neck injury. What a brilliant end to one of the best days of my life. Dad had fetched the car and we loaded up everything to go back to the flat. I was two and a quarter miles into the course but still with another 24 miles left to go.

I relived the first day when I was back at the flat, non-stop talking, excitement and amazement, as I reflected on the experience. Of course each day wouldn't be like that, the first day was extra special and unexpected. I kissed Dan goodbye when he reluctantly left us all to go to work, but Sue arrived so I got to tell the stories all over again. I was shattered but buzzing. I knew that I needed to switch off and to rest but my head was full of the most fantastic thoughts and memories from the day. Eventually I went to bed and I am certain that I fell asleep smiling.

It was going to be very hard setting out on day two. The second day couldn't have been more different from the first day. It was raining, hilly, quiet and a struggle to find a pub or café for a rest point. Les and Ian were the two essential helpers whilst Mum pushed Maisie along in the pram. Others soon gathered; strangers who had run the marathon came back to support me whilst they were still in London, and before I knew it there was a bundle of us walking in the Woolwich area of London.

Walking up the hills was taxing because I needed more tilt in order to get the foot clearance. The down hills were equally as demanding as the jarring in my arms and shoulders increased; each step caused me to slam my crutches down even harder. I had been told the London Marathon was fairly flat but it didn't seem like this when I had to rely on poor old Fred. I definitely noticed every hill, with their relentless demands, particularly when the majority of day two was spent either going up or down. My face dropped as I turned the corner to see another hill.

"Keep looking down, look at your feet," suggested Les. He didn't want me to see how far these daunting hills went on for. As soon as I was told not to look I made sure I managed to glance up to see the 'mountain' that lay ahead. "Bloody hell," I mumbled, "How far have I gone now?" Mum stopped and got the map out for what seemed like the hundredth time already and we had only got to the three mile point. I could walk for an hour and not be much further along on the map. A marathon was a very long way, especially in a robotic suit, but I kept telling myself every step got me a little closer to the finish.

I felt my face light up when Charlie had gone ahead and had found a café for us to go to. Of course I welcomed a break from walking, but it wasn't really a rest as the whole time was spent being interviewed by local papers. But I thoroughly enjoyed feeling refuelled and the hot drink to warm up.

It might not have been the world's most exciting challenge but the group we had made it thoroughly entertaining. We joked and laughed as I put one paralysed leg in front of the other. I wondered if this amount of fun would last for the entire Marathon. Maybe in a few days I would be feeling lost and lonely and people would forget about it, or at any rate they would until I was closer to the finish.

From the first day I ever stood in the suit I knew the marathon would be a mammoth undertaking but I hadn't considered all the other challenging tasks. Each day the journey across London, from our accommodation to the start of the day's marathon route was a long one, and taxi fares were over £50. We came to the end of a successful day two but finding a taxi wasn't easy. We all loaded onto a bus; the driver was awkward about all our equipment, but we managed to squeeze in. We got off at Greenwich station in the hope of finding a taxi, and our eyes lit up when we saw a few all parked up with their lights on. We wandered over to the first one and the taxi driver had completely the opposite character to the bus driver. He was the most helpful, friendly guy you could ever wish to meet. It took three attempts to fit everything into the cab, possibly the most anyone has ever got in one taxi. I explained what Fred and I were doing, as I am sure he wondered what the hell we had been up to. The cabbie's name was Dominic; he was instantly supportive and became our taxi driver and friend for the whole marathon. Bless him, he didn't even want to charge us, he just kept saying, "Donate it to the charity". Dom would collect us at the end of the day and take us back to the same spot the next day; he was always intrigued to see how far I had made it. He became an important part of the team.

The stairs in the flat proved to be another strenuous warm up before I set off each morning. It was easy when Dan was there to carry me but for the first few days there was just Mum, Maisie and Kate or Sue. I literally dived out my chair onto the first step and then I got up the others, one at a time, on my bum with a little help. Maisie usually started crying to add to the stress whilst I was doing this, and would then scream even louder as Fred was carried up the stairs. What a palaver!

It was a relief to get into Dom's taxi after a fraught start to the day. Even though everything tended to be more of a struggle when staying away because of things like stairs or bathroom layout, having Louenna's flat was absolutely brilliant.

By now, the papers and news broadcasters were picking up on my efforts and distance covered, and most days I had an interview. Walking and talking were so demanding and I found so many of my breaks were filled with question after question, not only about the marathon but going back to the day of my accident and even before. The more media coverage I got the more help it gave me to reach my target so I was accepting them all. Each day I would pass my phone to someone who would arrange these interviews and relay messages to me. I also had help from Spinal Research's PR agency, but many of the phone calls came directly to me.

One evening I was sitting in the flat reading the numerous encouraging 'tweets' and Facebook messages to spur me on. I then looked to see what articles had gone up. There was already an abundance of newspaper reports. I was deeply touched to see the support out there; in fact I was totally overwhelmed, until my eyes cast on a few nasty comments. There were thousands of very kind words and just a few spiteful ones, but these were enough to make me both cross and disappointed. I found it hard not to think about these negative remarks and in some ways I wanted to reply but they were doing it for a reaction so I ignored them.

"She is spoilt. Helicopter for her wedding, ski holidays, now the suit. It is all about money not her determination or work." I felt like explaining that the helicopter belonged to a friend, I worked for my skiing trips and wonderful friends enabled me to be able to fundraise for the suit. Other comments said I was, 'attention seeking, does she not realise she could complete it in a day in a wheelchair?' I think they missed the reason I was doing this.

"Stop reading them," said Mum firmly. Mums are usually right, so I didn't read any more, and I put these to the back of my head. I had so many positive words of encouragement on my 'Just Giving' page, so I read them and these gave me the boost I needed.

Kate could not stay for the whole time but came when she could. When she was not there Anna and Sarah, two friends living in London, offered their physio skills to keep me as pain free as possible. They would pop over in the evening. My arms felt sore as expected but the more I did the better they became; the first week was the worst. The mental concentration was exhausting and when my core fatigued I just became even more floppy. Once my body became a hindrance my arms took even more of a hammering, as I used them to hold my body upright. It was a vicious circle but it sent a clear message when I needed to call it a day.

I knew what I had to do and I wasn't surprised about the difficulties of walking along the London pavements. After 12 weeks' training I had a good idea of what to expect, but nothing could have prepared me for some of the events I witnessed. I was totally focused on what I was doing when I heard a voice: "It's that crazy woman from the paper". The voice had come from a homeless man; he put his can of lager down and got a fiver out to donate. Moments like this will stick with me for my entire life; there really are some special people in the world. His generosity made that mile so much easier. He made such a difference to that day.

Some evenings we had many friends and family with us so we would use Chancery Court. It was in fact easier for me as I could use the shower there and it was all accessible and, of course, I was very spoilt. Astrid even arranged a spa treat for me one evening. She also put together a rota for the hotel staff to come and join me pacing the streets of London each day. "Astrid, you are not making me want to complete the marathon in a hurry," I joked.

The rain didn't stop for days. I sat in the taxi staring out of the window at the puddles. "I really don't feel like it

172

today," I said. I felt low in energy and flat, not in the mood to strap the suit on and keep going. I sighed and told myself to get on with it. That morning was testing but, like most of the days, something would happen or someone would turn up and it would lift my spirits. As well as all of my lovely friends who came as often as they could, I also had high profile names joining me and supporting the challenge. This was a huge boost and it never failed to give me the energy and the desire to keep me going.

The day when I felt completely exhausted came the inspiration I so needed. Matt Hampson turned up to join me for a short time and he made the sunshine come out too. Matt was the best person to motivate me. I was doing this to raise money to help get a cure for paralysis. Matt sat there unable to breathe unaided, he used a ventilator. Of course completing the marathon was my short-term aim, but this reminded me of my ultimate goal. One day I shall see Matt and others get the use of their arms again and to breathe again without a ventilator. I had a book that I asked all the people who joined me to sign. Matt got the pen in his mouth and signed my book in better writing than mine. He never ceases to amaze me, but most of all he's great company to have around and he gave me the boost I needed.

Dan was back and could now stay until all of the 26.2 miles had been walked and the London Marathon completed. In his hands he clutched a few newspapers. He passed them over to me, "You're getting lots of national press". I started to flick through them. The Telegraph article was huge. "What the bloody hell is that?" I shrieked. There, spread across the page, was a photograph of me. I had never seen such a hideous photo. It hit you in the eye it was that noticeable, and it was massive. It was a picture of me standing in Fred wearing my waterproof trousers and looking like Mr.

Blobby. On the day the photo had been taken it was showery with sunny spells. As they were not easy to put on and take off I had kept the waterproof trousers on over Fred, but had taken the jacket off. My hips looked about double the size of my body. I felt like dashing out to buy every copy of the paper, which of course wasn't possible. The only option was to laugh. As a result thereafter, when I compared any photo with that one I was always pleased with it.

I had joined Twitter only for the marathon and it had taken me a while to really understand why I was advised to use it. I learned why when my waterproof trousers had torn, and a friend sent a tweet that I needed some new ones, preferably with zips. Within five minutes I had an offer from Farlows on Pall Mall. Dom did a detour on the way back to collect the XXL men's fishing trousers. I could now look my best on national television in my new huge trousers. That was the kind of support I was receiving regularly throughout the walk.

Cars and taxis were beeping in support, and as my friends carried signs with the 'Just Text Giving' code on people were pulling over to text donations. The money being raised for Spinal Research was constantly increasing. Friends were checking the 'Just Giving' website on their phones whilst we walked and were reporting the total to me as often as I asked to look at the map.

It was a pleasure to join Claire on her amazing journey through the streets of London, watching her determination to tackle the most horrendous weather, not only negotiating her robotic legs along uneven pavements and curbs but around huge puddles! It didn't just rain it absolutely poured. I was informed I had to look my best today as we were going live on TV. Wow, I get to meet the lovely Mark Bushell, the drowned rat look wasn't what I envisaged on my first TV appearance. I was nominated the brolly holder, watching Claire tirelessly struggle in and out of a HUGE pair of waterproofs for the umpteenth time to cover up Fred! They were very unflattering for her TV moment! However, I stood proudly by my friend as she gave a wonderful interview, smiling and feeling positive about what seemed her never ending challenge. Her interview was done and she soldiered on again. I am now on phone duty, it is constantly buzzing with either a phone call or text message, It was newspapers wanting interviews, or meetings. Blimey she's getting famous! The sheer generosity of people was overwhelming, in traffic jams people would be waving £20 notes out of their windows for us to collect; cars, taxis, buses were honking their horns shouting words of encouragement. Particularly in this current economic climate, I remember a little old lady was waiting for a bus and handed us a £20 note. We stopped for lunch in a little cafe in probably not the most affluent area and a young girl gave Claire £5, I couldn't believe how kind people were. Not once did we rattle our collection buckets, we didn't need to because total strangers were coming out of buildings, crossing busy dual carriageways and making every attempt to give Claire, whom they didn't know at all, money for her worthy cause. It really restores faith in human nature. It was an amazing atmosphere; I met some lovely people who walked with Claire on that day. I had a memorable day, despite the grim weather. I admire Claire for her determination and drive to succeed in this challenge and she always kept smiling. Georgina Sim.

The rain poured and the wind blew, brollies were turned inside out and I was almost blown over. I was focused on each single step, my arms were weary, my hands were sore, but I was still having the time of my life. The continuous horrendous weather caused most of the horse trials to be cancelled including the prestigious Badminton Horse Trials. By this time I was approaching the halfway point, crossing Tower Bridge with crowds of supporters walking next to me with banners, and TV cameras filming. I was joined by many friends from the eventing world, along with sports presenter Gaby Logan and her family. The atmosphere was once again electric, the noise of people shouting "Claire's Walk coming through," and tourists staring at this group of 'nutters' with a look of confusion as if to say, "What the hell are they up to?"

To reach half way was a very satisfying feeling, people started to believe I would make it and the word was spreading around London, leading to even more beeping from drivers and encouragement. We were all soaked by the end of the day; we finished the day in a restaurant on the North side of Tower Bridge. I could hear laughs and chatting. Everyone had thoroughly enjoyed what could have been a pretty miserable Sunday, including myself. The donations were coming in and the total was going up and up. It would soon be near £35,000. At this rate that ridiculous target I had set could possibly be achieved.

Fred was behaving impeccably; so far we had not had any problems with him, and he was new technology so it was as much a test for him as it was for me. I had a small rub just below my knee caused by a chafing strap but Kate had padded it up and prevented it from getting worse; my legs were in good condition. They hadn't walked for five years though and I did wonder if they ached but at least I couldn't feel them. In fact I felt they deserved to tackle a marathon after being so lazy for so long.

I had days when I felt particularly tired and weak, but on other days I was aware of how being upright, and making small flickers of activity by working hard, had made my core strengthen and my walking improve. Of course, I had always hoped that by the end of the marathon I would be like Forest Gump, and although that was unlikely, it was certainly strengthening me.

The sun was shining on to my control watch as I was standing outside one of the few pubs we passed. I could not see the LED display lights buttons clearly and thought I had pressed the walk mode. I heard three beeps, "Shit, help! I am sitting down. HELP!" I yelled. Luckily three friends ran in to hold me whilst I was in sitting position until the stool was unpacked from the bag and placed underneath me. Yet again we were all in fits of laughter.

I found it near impossible to switch off and give my brain a rest. In the evening I would read the messages I had received that day but the sheer amount of encouragement I was receiving meant I couldn't reply to each and every one, which bothered me. I felt rude and I did my best, but as each day ended I was becoming more and more worn out. Chancery Court had the remedy, a most luxurious spa area and my attempt to chill out was to go to the relaxation room. One evening Dan and I were stretched out on the comfortable loungers. It was silent in there and there were two ladies lying with their eyes firmly closed looking very relaxed. I lasted only five minutes before I gave the eye contact to Dan that I needed to leave. I had tried to copy the other women, I put in one hundred percent effort into relaxing but it was not working. I had such a busy head full of the jobs I needed to do and the emails I must send. We went back to the room and I ploughed through all my emails, from media requests to people asking about walking with me who needed to know where to meet us. I appreciated and wanted their company and the media were helping me to raise the money; it was essential that I replied.

On average I was covering approximately 1.5 miles a day, and I was now 14.5 miles into the marathon. I had just completed the highway which felt like it would continue into eternity, and the pavement had a noticeable camber. I was relieved when I got to the end of this road because to me, my legs had felt as though one was shorter than the other. It had been both difficult and uncomfortable. Then Dan broke the news to me that we would be doing the same road all the way back, great!

As a paralysed athlete who practises 'walking' in calipers daily, I was amazed that anyone would consider attempting the marathon. So after tweeting with Claire, my husband Pete and I organized a trip down to London to spur her on.

We met with Claire and her team in a cafe. Even after walking for 9 days, there was still a buzz of excitement around the group. The contrast between Claire in a wheelchair - a mobile and independent mother - and Claire on legs was striking. Every step in the robotic suit jarred, much of her weight goes through her arms and shoulders, balancing looked difficult and this challenge certainly wasn't something she could do alone. With both hands being used all the time, she couldn't even wipe her brow or scratch an itch.

Attempting to walk alongside Claire brought home quite how tough her challenge really was. I strapped on my calipers and with my husband Pete's help, pulled myself up on a railing and took my first few steps outdoors. Even the flattest of roads seemed dangerously uneven. Claire and Fred soon caught me up – I walked very slowly as Claire passed – "Cheers Anna, you are the first person I have overtaken on the whole journey," Claire shouted.

I managed to walk about 50m and spent the rest of the day in my chair, telling pedestrians and drivers about Claire's fundraising. Uncharacteristically, much of the London traffic stopped to find out more about the curious procession, shouted encouragement and donated generously! My favourite moment was when the London Fire Service edged past. They didn't carry cash, but stopped the engine, put on their fire suits and posed for a photo with us! It really brought home why I love Britain, an incredible day.

Anna Walford (Paralympian skier).

I had now made it to Canary Wharf, London's financial district. We were all very excited about the walk through here hoping to boost the fundraising to well above £50,000 to which it was very close already. I had never been to Canary Wharf before and it was like a different world. Around 90,000 people work there and as I walked along I was surrounded by modern tall buildings; a security guard escorted us through. It was very quiet with not a person in sight until lunchtime when smart looking people, all wearing suits, started to emerge. Rather to our surprise, as well as disappointment, there were not the donations that we had experienced in some of the less wealthy areas of London. Alec Lahore, from the eventing world, who worked for LOCOG, had arranged for some of the staff working there to come out of the building to cheer me on which was a great motivation. Lord Sebastien Coe also came out to meet me; who other than one of the world's best athletes could give me more or better encouragement?

Again I had much media coverage, as well as TV interviews. "Claire, can you go back up the road and walk that last bit again?" said one of the news reporters. It wasn't the first time I had to do this. Filming often took a long time and repeating the area I had just walked wasn't uncommon. This time was because they lost satellite reception in the area I was going through because of the tall buildings, but it was often because they just wanted a certain back drop. "Do you think 26.2 miles is not far enough?" I asked, but still managing to smile. Although I would rather not have had to spend the time repeating bits I reminded myself that all the publicity was raising not only vital funds for Spinal Research but also the profile of spinal injuries. I did not cover as much distance as I had hoped to that day because of all the filming.

When the story got out that I would not be receiving a medal from the organisers of the Marathon at the finish, I was constantly being asked how I felt about it. I had actually known for a while not to expect one. It was a new rule, if you didn't complete within 24 hours you would not be awarded the medal. I could understand this as I didn't have a timing chip in my shoe like the other athletes, so technically I could have cheated and not completed the whole course. I was told by Spinal Research a few months before my marathon and I must confess to having been just a touch disappointed, because to me a London Marathon medal on my wall had been something of a dream since my accident. However, I was not doing this for the medal, I had reasons that were far more important. It turned out the new rule was a blessing for my fundraising as it generated more and more press, and as this was happening I watched the donations pour in.

My overriding memories of my walk with Claire were a combination of factors throughout the day: the overwhelming support we received from the general public, the fun the group had trying to encourage passers-by to hand over some money and my lasting reminiscent point was seeing the look of determination on Claire's face as she took on the 26 mile walk just one step at a time.

I had watched Claire take those first few slow steps past the start line and hearing the cheers rise from the crowds lining the route was deeply poignant; I got chills watching her set off on what was inevitably going to be a life changing journey. I felt a sense of responsibility to support Claire in any way we could by giving her moments of laughter, strength and encouragement. I think I lost all the blood out of my arm as I held the umbrella over her and Dan to stop the miserable rain from getting into the suit.

On day 13 of her walk I headed into south east London to join Claire again at mile 21. The laughter we had that day was infectious, with some of Claire's closest friends accosting members of the public for donations and a policeman pulling up on his motorbike, not because of our raucous behaviour I hasten to add, but because he spotted Claire and wanted to donate. The display of charity I witnessed that day certainly evoked emotion, from cab drivers pulling over and people waving notes from car windows at traffic lights, to bus drivers opening doors to donate change and even an estate agent came out with £250 and a six pack of iron bru to keep Claire going.

I felt an overwhelming sense of pride following Claire's progress along her route. I can't put into words

clearly enough just how honoured I felt to be part of her awe-inspiring gruelling challenge.
Amy Bennett

"How am I going to cope?" I said to Dan. "I won't be able to stop myself crying." I was sitting in my room in the hotel discussing the last day's plan. I had completed the penultimate day leaving only three-quarters of a mile for the last day. It had been a tough day, and even though I had some fantastic company I felt like all my energy had been drained from me. I couldn't stop for breaks because I knew if I did I would find getting going again even more demanding. I did what I had to do and then called it a day.

I was expecting the last day to be emotional. Maisie was walking pretty well now so I was under pressure! We had BBC Breakfast and ITV Daybreak wanting to do an exclusive filming session on the morning of the last day but in the end we got both to film. It did however mean an early start.

The BBC arranged a taxi for us to go to the same spot where we had finished on day 16, at Westminster Abbey next to Big Ben, for my morning interviews. For once it was not raining, which was fantastic as I did not have to wear the waterproof clothing, and it was so much better for people to see the amazing high-tech equipment that Amit had invented. I had an ear-piece in and had a chat to Susannah Reid, who had joined me a few days earlier. It was very different doing live TV like this as I had to just look into the camera, unable to see who I was speaking to, also there was a slight time delay. I was quite nervous, but at the same time I loved the challenge; it was good to be out my comfort zone. I didn't mess it up.

Straight afterwards was the Daybreak interview with Dan Lobb who had also joined me on day 12. Then he had even very thoughtfully brought with him some delicious cake for Maisie and me. At the end of the interview I was delighted when Dan said he would be coming down to see me at the finish. It was still too early to do the last section of walking as I needed to finish at lunchtime for the live news, so we went back to the hotel to wait. I was feeling sick with anxiety.

I knew it was going to be an amazing day but not for one second did I realise exactly how remarkable it would be.

We loaded up the taxi for the last time. We were now experts and knew the exact order we had to load things in so it all fitted. It was busy in central London and our journey took us a little while. My stomach was full of butterflies. We drove around the corner by Big Ben and I saw crowds of people gathering.

"You will have to clear the area for me to walk," I said to Dad. I thought it was a normal busy day for London, especially being in a tourist area. "I think they are here for you," said Dad. Dad enjoyed joking around and attempting to wind people up. Was he just trying to make me even more anxious? Dom pulled over for us to unload, as we opened the taxi door I was greeted by cameras being shoved in my face. People around were waiting and everyone was there to walk the last part of my challenge with me. I tried not to look as shocked and surprised as I felt, telling myself to focus on the job in hand. I was put at ease knowing that Matt and Ian were back to help as well as Dan.

As the straps were being done up for the last time I whispered to Dan: "I can't believe this, it's just unbelievable." We were all taken aback by this, and it was essential we all kept our cool. We had to still pay full attention, to make sure that none of the straps were pinching me; we all kept focused on the job in hand.

How on earth had I got all this media attention? It was crazy; I had several microphones attached to me for interviews before I started walking. It was a good job I had twenty six miles experience as I had improved considerably at walking and talking simultaneously and it was evident on the last day. I was constantly having a microphone thrust in front of me to speak into, and questions fired at me. The hustle and bustle of the media frenzy was unbelievable. They were shouting at each other to get out of the way, some were even running on the top of a wall that ran alongside where I was walking. I felt a tremendous buzz generating. Was coming last in the London marathon really worth all this attention? There were celebrities there to witness my finish, some had been more than once: Claire Balding, Ben Fogle, Matt Holland, Matthew Pinsent to name just a few. My wonderful family and friends, new friends and even strangers clapped and cheered.

Behind me were three black horses; it was the Household Cavalry. My good friend Hannah had managed to arrange this, she had mentioned it but I didn't think it could possibly happen. I had to try my best not to be distracted or even think about anything other than tilting my pelvis correctly to take each step. With all this attention on me I didn't want to mess up now. I also knew how easy it would be to break down in tears if I started thinking about it; concentrating on the walking would help me to avoid this. To say it was overwhelming would be an understatement.

A memorable moment was when we all stopped for a minute's silence at the spot where Marathon runner Claire Squires lost her life competing in the same race only a few days earlier. She was only aged 30 and was also from Leicestershire. There were heaps of flowers and as I stood there tears welled up in my eyes. I was having a surreal day and this much-loved girl had died whilst also running for charity. Every one of us felt the profound sadness as we thought of Claire, her family and her friends.

As I turned to walk the last part down the Mall, I heard my friend Hannah shouting: "Look up Claire, see what is ahead." For a few seconds I took my eyes away from my feet to see a truly wonderful sight, it was the finish line. There was a red ribbon and an archway of red balloons organized by Spinal Research. I had almost made it.

Then Fred started beeping with one leg straight out behind me. "Matt, where is Matt?" I shouted in a panic. He soon arrived and we switched Fred off and on again to reset him. At that moment my heart rate was going like the clappers, surely nothing could go wrong this close to the finish line, with so much media to witness it. We all felt a huge sense of relief when I continued to walk. It was possibly interference from all the microphones that confused poor Fred. I was marching at what seemed a quicker pace now, the finish line was within throwing distance. The excitement built, the noise increased and my emotions started to show. People were showing their support as they were lined up each side of me.

Maisie was in front holding onto Sue and Sue's friend Helga's hands. She was beating me. I joked and suggested she walked behind me so it didn't look like I was last. She loved all the attention and was no doubt very proud of her newly found walking ability. I was hugely proud of her.

I had made it! I took that final step and the ribbon dropped to the ground, the crowds were gathered each side of me with all the cameras and press in front of me. It was as if it was a major sporting achievement, yet I had come last in the 2012 London Marathon. It had been a huge challenge to me but so was getting out of bed on those dark days, in fact that had been even harder.

As I stood there all I could see were hundreds of photos being snapped. A young boy ran over with a rosette he had made for me, and Charlie kindly presented me with his medal. After all that, I had been given a medal by someone who, during the 17 day marathon, had become a true friend. I could not hold back the tears any longer; I was overcome with a build up of all the emotions I had felt in the past hour. I hugged all my family, and was given a very special one by little Maisie, who didn't understand what all the fuss was about.

Holly Branson was at the finish line to present me with the Virgin Trophy, which is for people who complete superhuman feats of endurance. I was truly flattered that Sir Richard Branson thought I deserved this. It was something that I shall always value.

Spinal Research's team had somehow organized the media fantastically well, and that was no small feat. Their enthusiasm meant they were all very pushy and boisterous, so there had to be a strict order. The live news took priority, both nationally and my regional channel. After that it was one interview after another. I eventually sat down, and what a fantastic feeling it was. I had spent five years desperate to stand up and now I just wanted to sit down.

Then came another surprise. Matthew Pinsent presented me with a box full of letters and medals. He had tweeted to ask if any 2012 marathon runner would donate his or her medal, and the response had been breathtaking. For me this was better than the organiser's medal; these runners had earned their medal and I felt genuinely touched by people's abundant kindness.

Just as I thought I had done the last interview we saw a man speedily cycling towards us. Channel 4 News had heard something was going on in the Mall and had sent Jon Snow to investigate. He came over smiling with a friendly, warm approach. "How far can you walk without the suit?" he asked. "I'm paralysed, I can't walk," I replied. Jon was fascinated by the suit and my marathon, it was such a different interview it was refreshing.

I was told that my challenge was trending on Twitter, I didn't know what it meant but later found out that '#claireswalk' was one of the top ten things being talked about on Twitter at that time. I was impressed once again. I had never experienced anything even close to this.

Dom was there to take us back to Chancery Court where I had a celebratory party. Astrid and the team hosted a fantastic champagne and canapés party for me and also presented me with some gorgeous flowers. I recognized how truly incredible this was, considering I should have been giving them flowers for making us so welcome and letting us stay for so many nights. It was wonderful to have friends and family there to enjoy this moment with. For me particularly, it was still emotional; the tears rolled down my face again.

The very final interview for the day was a live one for BBC East Midlands news, set up in a room at the hotel. I was shattered and relieved to be finished after this. Now I needed some quiet time to myself. Sitting in my room, just absorbing what had happened and reflecting on the day, I started to look on Twitter and Facebook. I had so many messages. Sadly there wasn't time for me to read them all at that time because there were new ones coming in and pushing the older ones down. I would have to wait. I found it very difficult to concentrate on much at all. I was still excited but absolutely worn out. The amount raised was phenomenal, about £80,000; it was beyond my wildest dreams. I spoke to a couple of my closest friends who hadn't been able to make it to the finish but I was too tired to do much texting, speaking or social media. At the same time, I was far too hyped up to be able to sleep.

I had been invited onto Daybreak for the following morning and when Rachel from Spinal Research told me the taxi was at 6:30 am I was pleasantly surprised, as it had always been earlier for that programme.

Dan gave me a kiss and a cuddle to say well done and I too thanked him for walking behind me for much of the route, and again tears rolled down my face. We were both stunned by the whole day, in fact the entire Marathon. I was back to the same situation of the first night, I couldn't sleep and I desperately needed to, but how could I after the day I had just lived? I wondered what I would be doing if I had not had the accident. One thing was for certain: I wouldn't have just experienced anything quite like the past 17 days and shared them with the most special people in my life.

10

"Who can be sending a text message at this hour?" I asked myself, as I grabbed my phone off the bedside table to read the message.

"Bloody hell, shit! The taxi is here to collect me," I shrieked. Unfortunately I had been given the wrong time for the Daybreak interview and I was due to leave now. I had only had five hours sleep and a few more would most certainly have been very much appreciated. It surprised even me how fast a paralysed person could get up, be dressed, have a pee and out the door when under pressure. I barely had time to brush my hair though. Mum and Dan had also jumped out of bed and into their clothes just as quickly and the three of us were out of the room in a flash. We left Maisie to have more sleep as Dad was still there to look after her.

I wasn't sure I was ready for a live TV interview; I just hoped that the make-over would help me to look and to feel a little more alive. Dan hopped out of the taxi at Waterloo, as he had to go back to work, back to reality, although he was recognised on the platform at the station.

My experience in the ITV studio was somewhat different from the previous occasion. Mum and I were once more taken aback by everyone's response and genuine excitement. Again, it was as if I was a celebrity. I had my photo taken with so many people and there was a general hype about my achievement. I simply couldn't believe it. There were newspapers in the green room and there I was on the front page of the national papers. 'Dreamlike' best describes how it all felt. The fuss, attention, interest and excitement that the marathon had attracted I could never have anticipated for a second. I was being congratulated by Lorraine

189

Kelly and Mylene Klass when the make up lady called me into her room. I saw my face in the mirror and thought that no amount of make up was going to be enough to take away this look of total exhaustion, and my voice was husky from all the interviews I had done the day before. 'Never mind,' I thought, as I searched for something positive, 'it might encourage people to donate if I look worn out.' The last time I had been in this position, sitting whilst waiting for my interview, I had been a nervous wreck, but having been bombarded by interviews at the finish of my marathon I now felt quite experienced and confident. It is amazing what a difference a single day could make, to make me feel like a different person. I had gained so much confidence.

I loved being in the studio. There was a relaxed, cheerful atmosphere, and all the staff were friendly. My interview with Helen Fospero was a success as there was an influx of donations afterwards. In fact, throughout the day the total on the 'Just Giving' page rocketed. I realised that I clearly had not reached the maximum total yet.

I caught up with Helen after my interview and she told me about a charity she was a patron of. It was the Nicholls Spinal Injury Foundation. She had met David Nicholls a few years ago following his son's horrific accident that had left him paralysed from the neck down. Helen wanted to do what she could to help, so her involvement meant she understood the impact of spinal injuries on people's lives very well. Helen suggested that I should meet David and before I left we agreed to arrange a date for the summer.

As we approached the exit doors of the studios there were loads of photographers waiting and hovering. "Wow, there must be a famous person leaving the studio soon," I said in excitement to Mum. Naturally, I wanted to see who it was that was about to leave as I was convinced it was someone at the height of their fame, maybe a Hollywood star. We hung back for a while but after a long few minutes, I said, "Oh sod it. Let's go!" I was absolutely bowled over and taken completely by surprise when I discovered that it was me they were waiting for. It was so easy on such happy occasions as this, to smile for the numerous photos taken of me getting from the door into the taxi. I continued to smile and waved one of my marathon medals at them. It all felt so strange, so totally surreal. I knew that I needed to absorb exactly the scale of my marathon, but it was going to be quite a while before I got any time to myself.

We had everything packed all ready to leave the hotel and I felt very sad having to say goodbye to my new friends. I was just hugging Astrid and thanking her for her kindness when out of the corner of my eye I saw Hugh Grant. I felt like I was in the film Notting Hill, but to Astrid seeing stars like this was just part of her job. I had a photo taken with him and I confess that it gave me great pleasure when posting it on Facebook. People couldn't believe that I was meeting all these famous faces.

It was great to be back home and I was looking forward to having time now to unwind, when I heard a knock on the door. Mum answered it and came to tell me it was ITV Central news. I was lying on the bed resting my aching body and relaxing my tired mind. It upset me to have to say that I just could not give another interview just now. I looked a state and simply yearned for a shower followed by a good night's sleep.

I wondered how I was going to deal with what I believed would be a huge anticlimax after the marathon. It had been my ultimate focus for twelve weeks before the race day, during the marathon, and then a whirlwind of media attention, meeting celebs and making new friends. I expected to go home and to miss it all. It wasn't like that though because it just didn't stop. I had interview requests from around the world; The Middle East, China, Canada, and America. It continued to be wonderfully crazy.

I took advantage of most of the opportunities I could in the hope it would increase the fundraising, which it did. Each morning Dad would sit in the kitchen with a cuppa, delighted to see the total rising. Over the next couple of weeks it reached a phenomenal £210,000. I had definitely witnessed the incredible generosity of the public, and it encouraged me to continue to raise funds. I was not going to let this be the end, this was the beginning.

The interviews were very tiring and repetitive. It was a relief when they quietened down a little bit so that I could answer some of the other requests I was receiving. I was also already planning my next challenge. When Ben Fogle joined me during the marathon, he told me that I would want to do more after I had completed the 26 miles, and he was right. I was eager to do something else.

I gave it considerable thought and had an idea that might or might not work. I used my FES bike regularly as part of my rehab and found it fascinating to see my paralysed legs actively working. I had to take a month off using it both leading up to and during the Marathon itself. I could already see how much my legs had wasted in that relatively short time.

I sent an email to Derek at Anatomical Concepts to get his reaction to my thoughts. I wanted to do a cycle challenge powering a trike with my leg muscles and make this another world first. If I could cycle from Paris to London using the power from paralysed legs then it would be a pretty impressive feat. Derek sent me a positive response and they were willing to work with me to see if I could achieve this. The training had to begin immediately, building up the minutes spent on my static FES bike.

The media's most common question was, "What is next then?" So I wanted to have an answer whilst there was such interest and I thought using the technology of FES would give the papers and TV more to report on.

One of the many requests I received was to visit a special needs school near Leicester and I decided I should accept their invitation because if my marathon could inspire these young children then it would definitely be worth it. I felt quite nervous, I had no experience with disabled children and I spent the first five minutes experiencing a mixture of emotions. It is natural to steer away from disability and I found myself feeling very sad for about two minutes. I was alarmed by the severity of some of their conditions but this sadness soon passed. These kids were happy and this school was a magical place. I had two groups to speak to and this was one of the best days I have ever had. It was an experience that has changed me forever. I was surprised how uncomfortable I initially felt but this was soon replaced with total admiration for all the kids and the staff at the school. I shared many laughs with them. The children were fantastic and we had a question time at the end.

"Have you ever fallen out of the chair drunk?" asked a curious 13 year old boy. "It has been known," I replied, smiling. "What did you drink that night?" he inquired. I don't think it was the question the teacher was hoping to hear, but I found it highly amusing. We had a fantastic afternoon and the younger group enjoyed passing around and taking it in turn to wear a marathon medal. I had been asked to go in to inspire them as they had followed my marathon walk in the media, but I was the one who left feeling inspired by them.

Another visit was to Tedworth House to speak to injured servicemen. Again, it didn't take much consideration when I was asked. It was wonderful to have the opportunity to attempt to help these brave soldiers who had fought for our country. It was the most stunning of places in Hampshire, where the soldiers go after their rehab to try to get them to build up their new life. I spoke to them about my experiences since my accident and how I had gradually picked myself up from feeling at rock bottom. They asked me several questions and I hoped that I could inspire some, even if it was just a little.

My life was so different now and I had progressed beyond that point where I was at the centre of my own universe. I wanted others to enjoy similar progress and I often found myself thinking about other people's circumstances and problems. I was in the fortunate position of possibly being able to show them that life can turn around and they can get out of that dark place. I remember thinking that I could never be happy paralysed, it seemed impossible. I was wrong, and if sharing my story helped others then that is what I should be doing.

I was invited as a special guest to my home town's sports awards evening. Dan and I went along not knowing I was actually an award winner. I had a special achievement award. I was very proud and touched by this, and had a very enjoyable evening.

The bubble to my marathon success had never really burst. It had given me new opportunities, fresh impetus, and I was accepting as many offers as I could. It had not been so long ago when it felt like so many doors were being slammed in my face, now they were all flying open.

It would have been good to take Fred to some of the visits but the personal version was still not quite ready.

I was supposed to pay another £25,000 euros for my own suit, but after all the publicity and worldwide press coverage my marathon had got for Fred and for them, I felt it was unfair that I should have to pay the full price. I told Rewalk and Dave that I was not happy about that. After the marathon, I had continued to work on their behalf by answering emails from people enquiring about the suit and I expected them to be fair and to see that it was just not right to expect me to pay full price. Dave was not happy about giving me the suit at a discounted price but Rewalk were fantastic and said I did not have to pay any more. I was absolutely thrilled; soon I would have my very own Fred.

At this time Helen Fospero had arranged for David Nicholls and me to meet. I knew he was going to tell me about the research they were doing, but talks of this nature usually didn't excite me, in fact it often made me feel a bit deflated. I had been to an open evening that Spinal Research had put on in the past and although there was progression, nothing felt imminent. This time however it was very different. David Nicholls showed me the fascinating work that Professor Geoffrey Raisman was doing and for the first time I felt completely inspired by hearing about the research. It looked such positive work and I felt very optimistic about the future for spinal cord repair. I had always believed that one day there would be a cure but that chat with David made me think that maybe this is not so far away.

David is a top chef and businessman, he certainly does not lack drive and I admire all he has done and is still doing. It soon became very obvious to me that this was a charity I wanted to support. I had very much enjoyed working with Spinal Research and was pleased to have done so, particularly the raising of funds during the marathon. It was the right time for me to do whatever I could to support David and his charity. The Nicholls foundation has one major difference to Spinal Research in that David has a personal vested interest in research into spinal injuries. David has a paralysed son, so he shared the same passion as me about finding a cure for this life changing injury. I had already told Spinal Research about my idea of the bike challenge so I felt it would be wrong to change it to support the Nicholls Foundation. However I could raise money for both charities and that is what I decided to do.

It was August 2012 and my own Rewalk suit was now ready. I had another trip to Hull to have the settings all checked before I brought it home. When I first got in it the settings were wrong. It was too powerful. I couldn't stop. Even when I was being held by Matt my legs were kicking forward frantically, so it was adjusted and I tried again. We eventually found all the correct settings. It felt brilliant to have my own suit.

Whilst I was there I got a phone call from Freud Communications, who were doing the PR for the Paralympics torch relay. I was invited to be part of the cauldron lighting in Trafalgar Square in only seven days time. It wasn't going to be easy because I had to be in London the night before and I needed help with Maisie. Mum and Dad were on holiday so I had to see if they were able to look after Maisie on their return. I told Freud I would get in touch once I had spoken to them.

I had not quite realised what a massive opportunity this was. I thought I was one of eight involved and I had not understood what I was actually being asked to do. The Olympics had been such a success in London and I had enjoyed going to Greenwich to watch the Eventing team win their silver medal. The nation had loved the Olympics and we were missing the great sport on TV. The Paralympics were set to be the best ever, the tickets were selling out. To be involved in the start was such an honour. As soon as I knew I had Mum to look after Maisie I gratefully accepted the invitation and very much looked forward to being involved. When my torch-bearer's tracksuit arrived in the post and I was so excited about the day. I had a couple of phone calls with Dan from Freud and he said it was looking good for media coverage; it could be a big day. It never dawned on me exactly how huge this would actually be.

Dan and I went down to London the night before. We had a lovely evening with my physio friends who had helped throughout the Marathon, and we had an early night because our alarm was set for 5:45am. I had to be there so early to run through the procedures and to make absolutely certain that we knew what we were all doing. Thankfully we were lucky with the weather, it was dry. This meant I could use my brand new Fred. I wouldn't have been able to if it was raining as I had to be in the tracksuit, and could not have my waterproofs covering the suit.

I slapped on a bit of make-up and pushed myself in Percy up to Trafalgar Square whilst Dan carried Fred. Charlie also came along to help us. I met the team from Freud and I was given more information about what I had to do. "OK, you will walk in from here and over towards the cauldron. That is where Lord Sebastian Coe, Boris Johnson and David Cameron will be standing," Freud's Dan told me. "Are you bloody joking?" I asked. Oh my god, I was going to have to walk up to the cauldron in front of those three. What if I were to fall? My Dan would hopefully catch me but I would still feel embarrassed. I was also informed that it would be on Daybreak live, and filmed by many others, as well as all the press photographers snapping shots. At this point I realised what a momentous occasion this was, and I was the person lighting the cauldron.

I practised the walk so my legs weren't tight and I attempted to lift the torch. "Shit, it's heavy," I said. It felt even heavier for me because the very little core strength I had meant the weight of it pulled me forwards. I was told to take my time, which was inevitable because I didn't think I could have rushed it even if I had tried. Once they had lit my torch with the flame brought from Scafell Pike, I had to make sure there was a photo opportunity by just holding it for a while, before I attempted to light the cauldron. Everything was explained well and clearly but I was left feeling the most nervous I had ever been. I felt sick and just needed to get on with it, all this waiting was making me feel more anxious. I felt under pressure to get this right.

I had a live Daybreak interview about an hour before the actual cauldron lighting. Gethin Jones reminded me that millions of people would be watching this special moment. "Cheers Gethin, as if I am not nervous enough," I said, nervously laughing.

When David Cameron arrived, we had a short chat. I thanked him for the letter he had sent me after the marathon and he congratulated me again. I still couldn't believe what an occasion this was and that I was the one who'd been given the honour of lighting the cauldron. Then it all started and after Boris Johnson had spoken I was introduced. It was not very far to walk compared with what I had walked each day on the marathon but there was still plenty of time for me to catch a foot or lose my balance, particularly with all the audio and TV cables that were taped to the floor and looked like perfect tripping obstacles. Dan was behind me in case that happened but I actually made it over to the cauldron remarkably well. I focused on making sure I tilted my pelvis significantly and managed good foot clearance. My heart was pounding and I had butterflies in my stomach as I reached the cauldron. I was passed the torch and I held it firmly whilst it was lit, being supported by two people from the torch security team. This was the chance for the photo so as requested I took my time and looked over to the mass of cameras. I smiled but still felt petrified as I knew the challenging part was still to come.

I knew I wouldn't fall now, but to stand on legs that I can't feel was very difficult and I had to hold the long torch in exactly the right spot so I could balance it. It took a while. It was narrow at the bottom and wider at the top so my hands had to be in precisely the right place. "Down a bit," I said. "Up a bit," as they handed the lighted torch to me. It was quite scary not having my crutches because they help me to keep my body upright. They are my only contact with the ground that I can feel, and I felt naked without them. After struggling to get it right I finally felt I was holding the torch as well as I possibly could, so I went for it.

I noticed Boris Johnson was stood close to the flame, and I kept having terrible thoughts that his hair would catch light.

'Whoosh,' the Paralympic cauldron was now alight and Boris's hair was unscathed. It felt remarkable to be standing next to Lord Seb Coe, David Cameron and Boris Johnson and they were all clapping. I now had a genuine smile and felt relieved to have done it without any embarrassment. I was asked a couple of questions on the microphone and then it was all over. My heart rate returned to normal. I breathed again.

I felt on a natural high from all the adrenaline. I was then taken over to all the press for interviews and spent the next hour being asked "What did it feel like?" It was like the finish of the marathon all over again. I was touched they invited me to light the cauldron and I had one of the most memorable days in my life. Once again

I was reminded that if it had not been for my accident I would not have had this fantastic day.

I have had many spinal injured people contact me since my accident, and always I have tried to help each of them as much as I can by offering encouragement, advice and sometimes just listening and understanding. About two years before my marathon a young woman named Catherine sent me an email telling me she was still in hospital following a terrible car accident caused by skidding on ice. It left her with the same injury as mine. She was a lovely person and I visited her in Salisbury hospital and we became good friends. A spinal injury is bound to take some adjusting to but sadly Catherine struggled unsuccessfully to adapt to her new life and to add to it she'd suffered complications too. I'd spoken to her Dad and sister when she was having her darkest days so I felt quite involved and when I received a text from Catherine's sister to say that she had passed away, I was extremely saddened. I so wish that I could have helped her more. I shed many tears over Catherine's death and although my life had really picked up and I was as happy as ever, it hit home how spinal injuries can sometimes be such a different story. It wasn't many months before this when I had been in touch with a lady who also had a T4 spinal injury following a horse fall. In a message she said 'This is not living,' and then went on to ask me about the ReWalk suit. I did not realise that she was so depressed; she later took her own life. It is a sad but true fact that I can't always change someone else's outlook on life when they are paralysed. Also everyone's own circumstances are different, and this has a huge effect on coping with the injury. Some people cannot even return to their home because it is not accessible. I know my family and friends helped me get through it, as well as having the funds raised for the equipment. However, I learned from my early days of being paralysed that people can encourage and help but in the end it has to come from you. I spent a lot of time thinking about these two women and of others who are also suffering. I decided the best thing I could do to make a difference was to continue to raise awareness of spinal injuries and to raise money for the essential research into finding a cure.

I chose to do my cycle challenge in memory of Catherine, and I knew it would help me keep going when I lacked motivation.

I was increasing my FES time and my legs were certainly getting stronger, but they were also heavier from the build up of muscle. I was working alongside Derek, from Anatomical Concepts, and Andy, a physio who runs a rehab centre. Andy is an excellent trainer and he gave me a program to follow. I would keep the results I had achieved in each session. The FES bike had many readings that I could record such as power, gears and heart rate. It was encouraging to see my progress. I was waiting and looking forward to the arrival of the trike so that I would be able to put my hours of static training to use. I did have my concerns about how my legs would manage hills but this was unknown. We would just have to give it our best shot. It was brilliant to be working with another great company which was equally as enthusiastic as me.

I had also been nominated and invited to award evenings after the marathon, including Inspiration Awards where I was thrilled to win the 'Most Inspirational Fundraiser' category. The one that I felt most overwhelmed by was the Helen Rollason award for Inspiration at the Sunday Times Sportswomen of the year.

Dan was now working hard on his PGCE biology course, much to Henry's joy, because it meant he got to come with me to the awards. What made these awards so special was that we were surrounded by top athletes who'd enjoyed recent success at the London Olympics. To be in the same room as some of the women for whom I'd been screaming my support whilst watching them on TV going for gold was fantastic. I had so much respect for their achievements and was in awe of them.

We sipped champagne and chatted to a few people before we were called into the room where the awards would take place. "Claire, sit near the ramp in case you have to go up," said one of the organisers. It was at that point I thought I might be a winner. Henry looked at me pretending to be very serious and said: "You'd better win babe; I have come with you to see you win." We were sitting at the front and both of us felt nervous. "What are you nervous for?" I said to Henry. "I just am," he replied. My nerves were infectious. I don't know how many times I checked my feet were on the foot plates. Heels and foot plates were not a great combination. Also, when I have to stay still for a few hours my legs get spasms with any stimulation - such as the bump leading up to the ramp. This could so easily make my legs shoot off the foot plate and result in a struggle to get up, leaving me feeling stupid. I pulled my knees up to stretch my hamstrings in an attempt to settle them in case I was a winner.

Before the first award they played a short video with the highlights of 2012. There were snippets of Jess Ennis as she flew over the hurdles, Victoria Pendleton as she tore at great speed around the velodrome, Beth Tweddle who looked as supple as ever, and then me walking at snail's pace fixed into a robotic suit. Henry and I found it quite amusing to see me amongst all these unbelievable Olympians and Paralympians. The Helen

Rollason award was about halfway through, the fifth award of the evening.

When I heard: "She was an event rider and in 2007 she had an accident that left her paralysed...." I glanced at Henry to see him smiling. They were talking about me, I had won. I gave my feet one more check before I cautiously pushed myself onto the stage. It was deeply emotional for me and even Henry, who rarely cries, had tears in his eyes. What made it even more mind blowing was that I was given a standing ovation. I was in a room full of top sportswomen and there they were standing and clapping for me. I just couldn't believe it. I was presented with my award by Sue Tibballs from the Women's Sport and Fitness Foundation and was asked a few questions, which of course was the perfect chance to plug my next fundraising challenge.

To me, the Helen Rollason award is particularly special because Helen was such an extraordinary lady who tackled cancer so bravely and raised an incredible amount for charity, so to have an award with her name on it has to be the one that means the most.

Straight after being presented with the award I was whisked off for a Radio Five Live interview before I was back with Henry to watch the last few awards. We chatted to some of the medallists before we left and it was great to have them congratulating me, as I was congratulating them. Unbelievable.

Amongst many of the letters I received in the post following the marathon was one from Sheffield Spinal Unit. The consultant congratulated me on my achievement but also added he had read a few negative comments in the press regarding the care at the hospital. He said that it might not be anything that I had said, but if I thought that they were true he would like to discuss them at my next appointment, so as to possibly help future patients.

It was time for me to go for my annual check up, and although it was quite a while after I'd received the letter, I anticipated bringing up how I felt about the rehab. So, at the end of the appointment I reminded him about the letter and his request that we must discuss these comments. I confirmed that the care was exceptional and that I couldn't fault it, but I went on to tell him my experiences of the rehab. Three 45 minute sessions a week weren't enough for me. I informed him how being told that my legs would waste but they were of no use anyway was neither the information I wanted to hear, nor the negative attitude I thought should prevail. It also showed that they didn't believe research would develop a cure. I explained why I left and it was interesting to hear what he had to say in response.

Apparently there was limited funding which in turn limited the amount of physio patients could have. Since I was there this had improved and they were working on getting even more physio time in the future. They have to protect patients from seeking treatments that are offered in some countries and that are clearly dodgy. I understand this, and also that after a sudden devastating injury people can be very vulnerable. Also, to some extent, I do agree that what they advise about getting on with your life as it is now could lead to more happiness, rather than simply dwelling on recovery. However, the point I needed to make was that they should treat each person as an individual and to realise that for some, hope is good; indeed it is essential. It was hope that had kept me going through the early days. The physio and rehab I have done since have helped me become stronger in my core, have kept me fit and healthy. A combination of rehab and rebuilding one's life must surely be the best option.

I hope that our chat helped him to understand my view and why I discharged myself so early. I also hope they realise that 'hope' needn't be called 'denial'.

11

I felt despondent and frustrated. I knew that my face mirrored these same feelings; it was very similar to when I was doing some of the early rehabilitation. It was no wonder though for I had been spending hours every day on my static FES bike, so as to gain the additional fitness and strength that I would need in order to pedal my new trike when it arrived. It had been utterly boring cycling in my bedroom, all on my own, but the effort was showing encouraging improvements. My legs were powerful and I hoped that all this solitary mind-numbing hard work would mean that I would soon get to pedal the trike outdoors, including up and down hills, in the fresh air.

I'd been waiting quite a while for the trike to arrive and when finally I heard it was on its way from Germany, I was very excited. It was packed in a huge wooden crate and the carriers had offloaded it, leaving it with one side against the wall. When Dan started to remove the packaging we noticed a huge crack. The cracked side of the box had been against the wall. Dan used an electric screwdriver to get into the box but once it was open it was plain to see that the carriers had put the fork-lift through it and had damaged my trike in the process. I was absolutely gutted.

By now I was losing my motivation with the static bike training because I still had no idea how my legs would respond either to hills, or actually just cycling along the road. I had waited such a long time for this trike to be delivered. Each day that I plugged myself in for another long session on the static FES bike was just more time for me to doubt the challenge I had set myself.

Eventually I got another trike but it came with more disappointment. I just didn't see the response I was hoping for. My legs were moving erratically, looked too far apart, and my knees appeared to be unstable. I worked with the German company, Hasomed, who make the FES system, and with Andy to get it right. The trike was similar to the suit in that it was not something that had been used a lot so there was not much experience to fall back on. We all kept on trying and I made myself continue the tedious training on the static bike each day. Hasomed and Anatomical Concepts were as keen as I was to give this our best shot, and they were trying their hardest to get this working more effectively.

I knew this challenge would be really tough because getting my legs strong enough to cycle from Paris to London would be more demanding than for an able-bodied person taking on the task. My legs were working only whilst using FES, the rest of the time they were just paralysed legs doing absolutely nothing, so I would have to put in hours of work to make this achievable. The FES would only make my legs cycle if they were strong enough, so once they fatigued they would gradually stop. I knew I would find this irritating because no matter how much my mind wanted to do it, this would not influence my legs turning the pedals. This was a concern to me. However, despite the fact that things were not going smoothly, I didn't like to be beaten and we continued to try to make it possible.

I received an email from a woman named Jo Wyeth. She was a P.E. teacher at Brockington College, a school near Leicester. Jo asked me if I would consider coming to her school to talk to the pupils. She said the school would fundraise for my cycle challenge, and could certainly raise over £3000 by having a fun-run and a non-uniform day. Even though I was apprehensive about speaking to large groups of people, I couldn't let that stop me. It would be a fantastic start for my ongoing fundraising so I made the decision to go for it.

I had also been contacted by the producer of ITV Tonight, and they were making a programme on the Best of Britain 2012, which was to be shown on TV just before Christmas. I was flattered that they wanted to include my achievements in a year that boasted both the London 2012 Olympics and the Queen's Jubilee. When I spoke to them it seemed an ideal chance to make people aware of the next challenge. We decided that filming my school talk at Brockington College was a great idea too, and they could film me chatting with the pupils about the Olympics and Paralympics.

It was my first talk to a large group and I was being filmed by national TV as well as the local BBC news. Of course it was intimidating, but I decided that I must thrive on the pressure because I found myself in many situations like this.

As soon as I arrived I met Jo, and she showed me where I would be speaking. Sue and a member of staff helped carry Fred to the hall. As Jo and I were heading to the hall we passed a girl, who slowed down and looked overcome then muttered, "It's Claire!" "Hi," I said smiling at her. It felt really odd, but she had watched the marathon updates on TV and looked genuinely star-struck. I couldn't get my head around this; all I had done was walk slowly around London; the money raised had come from the thousands of people who had kindly donated.

Although at the time it felt horrible and once again I felt nervous, I convinced myself that this would help me do a good talk. I obviously like to challenge myself and put myself out of my comfort zone. It was something I missed in the first few years after my accident.

All the cameras were in place, and the kids started to fill the hall. I was standing tall in Fred ready to start my talk, with hundreds of pairs of eyes all focused on me. I was terrified. Occasionally my blood pressure drops when I stand, so I made sure I had plenty of time to adjust to standing. I had made a few bullet points but I intended to speak from the heart. I was not keen on reading any notes but a few points would be helpful if I lost my way.

The head teacher introduced me and I started by showing a short video, which a friend had put together, that included many aspects of my life. Then I told the children my story. I could not believe the attention I was given; you could hear a pin drop. They were all listening and looked as if they were taking in everything I said even though they were highly excited about the TV crew being there. For me it was just like leaving the start box on a cross country course, or skiing off from the top of a tough slope. Once I started my nerves vanished. It was quite remarkable that something I once hated was now something I loved. As soon as I began I enjoyed it, and I had so many questions afterwards which made me think that the pupils were genuinely interested.

"How did you stay motivated?" "How did you make yourself do things when you were feeling depressed?" "What was it like walking in the suit?" "How did you keep going for 17 days?" "How does the suit work?" These were just a few of the questions I was asked. It was fantastic to see the youngsters so intrigued.

I explained why I felt so lucky, as I had the use of my arms, and many spinal injured people lose their movement in their arms too, some are even on a ventilator. I also told them how a spinal injury affects almost everything from the injury level down; bowel, bladder, temperature regulation, blood pressure, sensation, bone density etc.

"This is why I am doing my cycle challenge. A cure must be found for this devastating injury."

Jo organised the optional fun-run, and over 90% of the pupils got involved. I had messages from pupils on Twitter after my visit; they were so keen to help raise money, and their enthusiasm was such a boost for me. "You have changed the way I think." "You are inspirational, I want to help," and "I have learned so much today."

I was stunned by their reactions and it made me want to continue to visit schools. I made another trip over to Brockington College to watch the kids do the fun-run and Maisie enjoyed seeing the kids run laps of the school grounds. It was fancy dress and what struck me were all the smiles these kids had on their faces whilst raising money for a fantastic charity. As they ran past me they waved and shouted how many laps they had done. It was a pleasure to see even the less sporty ones getting involved and enjoying the running.

My visit to Brockington ended up having a huge influence on my decision for the next fundraising challenge. I didn't have any other schools to compare this with and what I didn't know then was that Jo was a very special teacher, as without her enthusiasm and organisation this wouldn't have happened. She told me my talk motivated the children and she had never seen a response quite like it, but it was Jo to thank - it was she who made it happen. The school raised an impressive £7000 towards my cycle challenge. Jo has since become a great friend and training partner.

We still hadn't got the FES bike working well enough on the road and time was fast ticking by. I was still doing interviews and generating media interest; both were vital if I wanted to raise a lot of money again, but I was starting to doubt whether this challenge was going to happen. It was hard to explain to people what I was about to undertake when deep down I felt it was unlikely to be ready in time; I needed to adjust my schedule and have a rethink. Although in some ways it felt like the final straw, my mind was actually made up for me when I found out that fundraising in France was going to be nigh on impossible. We were not allowed to collect money on our journey in France for a charity that was not based in France. This made my decision for me. Now I knew it would be better to stay in the UK where my marathon had been given huge coverage and I could raise more money here. And so the new challenge was born.

After the success at Brockington College I decided that I should combine the cycling with school visits. Not only would this raise money for the charities but it would also, hopefully, have the same effect on other children as it had at Brockington College. I spoke to Charlie who was going to be a key member of the team and he agreed this was a much better idea. In fact everyone I mentioned it to thought it would work well.

The other big change to my challenge was going to have to be my giving up on the idea of FES cycling. We were nowhere near close enough to getting the cycling efficient enough for me to manage the distance and hills that I wanted to achieve. In some ways it was a relief, although I remained as keen as ever to show off the clever technology of FES.

Whilst I was visiting the rehab centre at Tedworth Hall I had spotted several hand-bikes. I emailed them to ask if I could borrow one to train on and they kindly let me. I'd had the bike a few months before I'd decided to alter the challenge, so I had used it a little. Ever since my accident I had always been a bit cautious about doing sports that require a lot of strength and repetitive use of my arms. I was ever conscious of the serious consequences so I did not want to over use them and cause injuries. My arms do everything for me; they are needed to lift my legs every time I transfer from car to chair, chair to shower or bed etc. It was vital I looked after them and treated them with utmost care. I was also worried that I might have massive upper body strength and a masculine, muscular look. Nevertheless I was desperate to do this challenge and I started training five times a week on the hand-bike. I found it extremely hard work and my first few rides were only five miles and I still needed a few breaks up the hills. I knew that to manage my 400 miles hand-cycling challenge, it was going to mean six months of hard training. The bike felt fantastic though; it gave me a feeling of freedom, similar to skiing. I had now found my summer sport which I had been longing for.

I gradually built up the distances, and tackled some steep hills. If I overdid it I got a pain in my elbows, but as I built up my strength the less the pain became. This challenge was going to be almost a marathon a day for three weeks, including two school visits most days and media interviews. In many ways the prospect was really daunting. Not only was the cycling extremely demanding but I had now given enough talks to realise how exhausting this was, particularly since it was essential I treated each talk like my first one, as I had new audiences to inspire.

I was excited about the challenge, but I also knew that there was a lot of work to do before then, not just the training but also the route and scheduling the school visits. During this time my Hotmail email account was blocked and I lost many contacts and lots of important information, which only added to the work load. Even after many long and frustrating phone calls to Hotmail Customer Services I never managed to get the email account back.

It was all made slightly easier because I found a child-minder for Maisie. Wendy lives in the next village, and had my friend's daughter three times a week. She rarely has any spaces for new children because she is exceptional but I'd heard she might have one. Maisie was now of an age where she needed to play with other children. It meant my longer cycle rides could be when Maisie was with Wendy, and Mum would help out at other times. Wendy even picked her up and brought her back to make it easier for me, and the children would regularly be taken to parks, soft play or swimming. It worked so well and meant I had time to get plenty of training in, but I still had lots of time to do things with Maisie. I was always very aware how important it was because the years go by too quickly.

Freud Communications PR Company had contacted me a couple of times, once in regard to the Paralympic torch lighting and the other was after the marathon when the press reported that there would be another challenge. I remained in touch with them and now they wanted to have a meeting with me to discuss the cycle challenge. I was not totally sure how they were going to be involved but I would learn this in the meeting.

They were a brilliant team and four of us sat around the kitchen table discussing the plans. Afterwards I was absolutely delighted when I got a phone call from David, who worked for Freud Communications PR, with an offer I simply couldn't refuse. Just-Text-Giving by Vodafone wanted to use my cycle fundraiser as an example of how much could be raised by text giving, a free service that Vodafone offer. They would provide all my clothing and printing, a lot of help with the planning

214

including the route, the PR and a donation which would help with expenses during the challenge, as well as a donation to the charity. I did have a few small concerns though. I had enjoyed doing a lot of my own media for the marathon and being in control. Having Freud involved would be different, it could change it. I also had the pressure of knowing Vodafone were watching all my interviews and that I had to make sure I mentioned Just-Text-Giving each time which, was very understandable. The positives outweighed the negatives and it was such a fantastic opportunity.

The cycle challenge was somewhat harder to plan. I was given a map for the marathon with the route to follow but this time we had to make our own route and schedule for the whole three weeks. Through email and word of mouth, I found schools that were keen for me to come and visit, and who would participate in fundraising. I had been given support previously from Advance Performance in Peterborough, a sports shop, owned and run by Sam. She had a contact at Marriott Hotels and kindly arranged a meeting with them. We told them about the challenge. It was wonderful news when they confirmed that they wanted to be involved, kindly offering two rooms each night of my journey. This led us to base the route around where the Marriott Hotels were, and which schools I would visit. Freud arranged the route to be devised using the expertise of people who helped do the Olympic torch relay route. This relieved me of this job and freed me to concentrate on training, media interviews, and talks, as well as being a Mum.

Everything was coming together with the help of the team from Freud, and I was pushing on with my training. My arms were not designed to get the weight of the hand-bike and myself up hills, and it certainly felt like that. Sometimes each turn was physically painful. I would set myself twenty rotations of the pedals and rest, and then go on again, determined to make it to the top. My training went on throughout the snowy, cold winter. There were days when I knew it was crucial for me to train, even when the snow was lying on the ground. I was feeling warm and cosy as I looked out the window but forced myself out to cycle. I ensured that I had enough layers on to keep warm, just like a day's skiing, but sometimes my fingers were so cold they were agony.

I roped in many friends to be training partners; the hand-bike was low to the ground and even with a flag attached to the back it was much safer to cycle with a friend, and also made it more fun. It was a help to have such reliable friends and I knew I was fortunate as they motivated me. We always found things to laugh about too as we cycled around the Leicestershire countryside.

Jo had not done much cycling and started training with me. By then I had already been training for a few weeks. It was a miserable day with a strong wind to make it even more demanding, the first time Jo decided to join me. I was cruel enough to take her on a long ride up some steep hills but I was kind enough also to give her a shorter option, but she didn't want to take that. I never heard the last of it, she moaned about her stiff legs and sore bum.

"Just be grateful you can feel your legs and bum," I would say, with a smile. Jo muttered some obscenities at me. After this I will never know how we became such good friends, either she was a forgiving person or she was also up for a challenge.

Mum had hardly ridden a bike but she also started cycling, as did Sue. I had a long list of friends and family I would send a message to as I planned the week's cycling, and I developed a weekly training schedule.

Sport has an amazing ability to give you more energy and I could feel my fitness improving by the week. The cycling was different from the marathon, and I definitely needed the six months training to strengthen my arms and become fit enough.

I also found the cycling to be relieving when I had back ache, and it was brilliant rehab as the slight bit of muscle I had in my abdominals was encouraged to work and this had to be good for my core strength. My arms and shoulders did not bulk up as I had once feared they might. They were certainly toned but did not look huge and bulky probably because I was doing endurance training.

There were some days when I felt knackered even on a short ride, and I was then seriously concerned about the cycle challenge. On other days I would be bursting with energy; I felt then that I could tackle anything. I imagine any athlete in training has good days and bad days; this is just a part of it. You just have to fight and keep on going when it gets tough.

I knew hand-cycling was a sport I would continue to enjoy after the challenge and I needed my own bike. I emailed two hand-bike companies in the UK, I explained what I was going to do and the media opportunities. Both were happy to give me a brand new hand bike so I had to make a decision which to go for. Then one of the suppliers offered me a brand new wheelchair as well, which I was getting desperate for, so this made it an easy decision. My new bike, and a replacement chair for Percy, were ordered from Quickie.

I had planned a skiing holiday but I felt I could not risk injury, so I didn't go. Not only because of all the hours of work I'd put in, but also because I felt I owed it to Vodafone, Quickie and Freud to complete this fundraising challenge. If I had gone I would have been ultra-cautious and that was not a good way of tackling a sport. The girl who had crashed into me just before my marathon training had made me realise how close that was to preventing me from achieving my dream. I did not have the chance to feel deprived though because I was so busy. It was the right decision.

Freud offered me some media training which I welcomed, so I grabbed the opportunity and had another visit to London. I always loved having a reason to go to London. I had grown particularly fond of the city after the marathon. The trainer and I looked back at old interviews I had done and she was complimentary about them; this was a confidence boost. She told me not to change a thing, which I felt quite flattered about. I was not expecting to hear that. We did some practice interviews, learning how and when to fit in the Just Text Giving line and I found that helpful. Working with Freud and Vodafone was great fun and although they were always very professional we had many laughs and I enjoyed working with them.

I had more school visit requests than I could fit in on the challenge so I arranged some to be fitted in during the period leading up to the start. All of them kindly participated in fundraising for the challenge, but I discovered that teachers like Jo were rare, and few people have either her kind of motivation or her 'can do' attitude. On the whole though, the schools responded very well and raised vital funds for the research charities.

Brockington College had a phenomenal total to beat. I really wanted the other schools to organise an activity the kids could take part in to raise money, as part of my talk was to try to inspire the pupils to be active and show them that even though two-thirds of my body could not move I had still found so much I could do to stay fit and healthy. I felt really chuffed when I received emails from the schools with photos of the children participating in sporting activities, all proud of their achievements and rightly so.

The mother of a girl to whom I'd given riding lessons a couple of years previously kindly nominated me for a 'Tesco Mum of the Year' award. I made it through to the short list and was then been invited to interview. Shortly afterwards I received a phone call to tell me that I was the winner of the 'Courageous Mum of the Year' award. It came about because of all the fundraising I had done, as well as being a Mum, and for me, it was a huge honour to be a winner. It was a real bonus to be involved in the most fantastic weekend break from cycling and being a Mum. There were only six weeks left to go to my challenge when I went off for this wonderful, glitzy awards ceremony.

I had met the other winning mums a few weeks before at a photo shoot for Tesco Magazine and we were all very excited when we arrived at the Savoy in London. I had special permission to come with a friend so Shane got to experience the luxury of the stunning Savoy Hotel. The first day was spent being pampered, having rehearsals and chatting with the other mums. Channel 5 was filming the awards; there was a real buzz whilst we prepared for the ceremony and I was quite nervous.

We had to come out on the stage as our names were read out. The ramp wasn't steep but again I worried about my shoes staying on the footplate and my leg spasms. I had several practices which were fine but I was still worried. It was Sunday lunchtime, the room looked absolutely gorgeous, as you would expect in The Savoy. Mum, Dad and Dan were seated at a table. They and Shane had been to a drinks reception whilst I was having my hair and make-up done.

The other mums had truly fascinating stories to tell,

and I was humbled by their achievements, Margaret Aspinell in particular. She lost her son in the Hillsborough football disaster and had fought for the truth for years. Margaret and I got on really well and she made me laugh so much. Apparently Margaret never usually wore make-up, and having hundreds of photos taken was not something she was comfortable with. "I can't wait to get this crap off my face," she said. I later found out she spent hours trying to get black mascara off in the shower. Before we entered the room full of people, including our families and celebrities, we were whisked off to the red carpet for more photos. It was only two and a half years earlier when I didn't want any photos taken at our wedding. It just proved how my confidence had grown in that short space of time. I still had moments of feeling self-conscious but nothing like I did back then. If I started to feel embarrassed about being in a wheelchair I just told myself that I wouldn't even be at this incredible awards ceremony if I'd not had my accident. I would have probably still been doing exactly what I was doing before my accident. Being paralysed had certainly changed my life and it now wasn't all bad. I had some fantastic perks and being picked out as a winner for this award along with these women, all of whom I greatly admired, was one of them.

We all waited behind the scenes ready to be called on to the stage. I wasn't the only one worrying; one of the mums had heels so high that I think she should have been equally concerned about getting up the ramp successfully. As I wheeled up I noticed Mum was already in tears, I knew then that this was going to be another emotional day. My friend Becky had Maisie for the day and I got regular updates on what antics they were up to, including riding Becky's daughter's pony, Bryan. This award was particularly special because being a mum is the best thing in the world.

We all enjoyed the scrumptious lunch followed by the awards. I was last of the eight awards given out so I felt a bit on edge throughout the whole ceremony. So many of the stories reduced me to tears, which I thought may have ruined my make-up that someone had spent ages applying. The room was full of emotion.

Eventually it was my turn, and the cameras turned towards me. A short video that Channel 5 had made was shown on a big screen. They had interviewed a few of my friends and my eyes filled up again listening to them talk about my accident and the marathon. It also included an interview with me and little Maisie appeared on it. I felt so proud of her. As I went up onto the stage everyone stood up, clapping for me. There were many well known faces including Celebrity Mum of the Year, Melanie C, Denise Van Outen and Louis Smith.

I whizzed up the ramp amazed by the loud applause I was getting, and the cameras moved along with me. Then, as I feared, my legs spasmed strongly, and I struggled to get to the top. Just as the host, Fiona Phillips, was about to help me, my legs settled and I continued. It was such a relief, otherwise it would have looked like I had not got enough strength to get up a small slope, just before I was going to tell everyone that my next challenge was to hand-cycle for 400 miles. This was another fantastic opportunity to publicise the cycle challenge and to raise awareness of spinal injuries. I was told they had a special message for me to watch. Sir Richard Branson appeared on the screen to say congratulations; it was such a personal, friendly message and I was really touched by it. Now, for what was the umpteenth time, I couldn't believe this was happening to me.

I was thrilled that my award was presented to me by my now friend and TV presenter Helen Fospero, and Rav Wilding. The whole weekend was perfect. We stayed a final night at the Savoy. Shane went home but Dan stayed and we just relaxed in one of London's poshest hotels. It was a lovely treat for Dan, as well as for me, because it had been a difficult year in some respects. Dan was in the thick of his PGCE course, training to become a biology teacher and we had had very little time together so this was a chance to relax together after a thoroughly exciting day.

We had one last surprise, before leaving to go home with heaps of gifts I had been given. On the Monday morning we all went to 10 Downing Street to have a nosey around and a cuppa with David Cameron. There was strict security to get in and we had all been told to bring our passports. We then had photos taken outside Number 10 before going in for our tour. It was pretty impressive in there as you would expect, and we all had a chat to David Cameron who was very easy to talk to. I asked him if he fancied joining my cycle challenge and it looked like he would if he could, but obviously he was a busy man. Dan and I left to go home with memories that would stick with us forever.

I felt tired and getting back into training felt harder after three days off. I dragged myself out on the bike and soon got back into it.

Not all the messages I received were up-beat or supportive. Prior to the cycle challenge I received messages, all from spinal injured people who knew each other. They had read some recent articles about me. According to them I was doing little to help get a cure for paralysis, and I should not be saying I had my best days after a spinal injury because this would not help research. One girl even said, "Are you serious that you can have the best days of your life following a spinal cord injury? No bladder or bowel function, no sensation and unable to walk."

222

I couldn't believe what I was reading. They were getting quite nasty about what I was doing, and I found it hard not to let it bother me. Did they really think if I looked miserable on the interviews that it would make people donate?

Perhaps they were very unhappy in their lives, but some of the most special days of my life have been after my accident and they could not see that as being possible. I was on a mission to help get a cure and raise awareness of spinal injuries, and it was hurtful to get such negative messages. They followed me on twitter, which I found quite strange if they hated what I was doing. I blocked them and forgot about them; instead I focused on the challenge that lay ahead of me.

Jo and I had organized a pre-challenge training session at Rutland Water. It was two weeks before I started the big cycle ride and we thought we could encourage people to join us, raise some money and generate some regional press. We decided to make it optional fancy dress and we were joined by about 80 cyclists, many of whom dressed in funny outfits. I was interviewed by my regional news and BBC Breakfast, plus lots of filming with Getty, who Freud had managed to get to film a few days of the actual challenge. There was a lot of stopping for filming like the marathon, but I was eventually free to cycle.

I felt exhausted cycling. I think so many interviews had used a lot of my energy, so I knew that two school visits a day, cycling and press interviews for three weeks was going to be highly demanding, but I was up for it. The training was over. I was ready to take on the hectic three week schedule.

12

It was 22nd April, exactly a year since I took my first step over the start line of the London Marathon. I was now undertaking another test of stamina and strength, both mental and physical. It was going to be a long day. Kate and I had stayed in Nottingham the night before because we had an early start. The alarm went at 5:30 a.m. I slapped on a bit of make-up and put on my branded clothing. We were soon heading towards Nottingham Trent University where the challenge would begin.

A friend who was a lecturer at the university had arranged this, and we all enjoyed breakfast there. Well, except for me, who seemed to have very little time.

This was different from the marathon, where there were thousands of people taking part in that. The atmosphere then almost made me run, never mind walk. This would be quieter and yet in some ways it felt more pressured. Expectations were high following the marathon success, and I was desperate to do a good job for Freud and Vodafone. I also knew that the marathon fundraising total was going to be hard to get even close to.

The Freud team members were very efficient and had put together a tight timetable of interviews for me. I was simply pointed in the right direction at the correct time. It had generated much media interest, not only local but national as well. This would boost the fundraising significantly and, of course, also continue to raise awareness of spinal injuries.

Quite a gathering built up to wave me off, and there were about 30 of us on bikes cycling to the first school visit. Mum and Dad had brought my bike over for me. Mick, our support-vehicle driver, was there; his role was to meet us at various points on the route with supplies and technical support if required. He later became known to everybody as 'Where's Mick', as our support vehicle driver. Sturgess's garage in Leicester had kindly lent us the vehicle for the duration of the challenge and a local business had kindly lent us a box trailer which was full of bikes, including a spare hand-bike, which proved to be very popular.

Once all my interviews had been completed inside the university I gave a short speech and thanked everyone who had come to see me off. By now, adrenaline was pumping around my body and I was eager to get stuck into the 400 mile cycle ride.

I wheeled outside and with a little help transferred myself from my wheelchair onto the hand-bike. My last interview before I left was BBC Breakfast and it was live. I got into position and, although I still felt nervous, it was so much easier than it had been just over a year earlier, when I'd given my first live interview on Daybreak.

"Remember the 'Just Text Giving by Vodafone'," said Becca. "They are all watching at Vodafone," she said and smiled at me, in a way that said 'Please do not mess this up.'

You never quite know what questions the interviewer will ask so it was essential I weaved in what I needed to say early on in the interview, and once I had done that I could relax. I was thrilled when Becca reported back to me that Vodafone were pleased with the coverage, and that there were quite a few donations whilst I was on TV.

Charlie led the way on the bike. Freud had given us a GPS but it wasn't working so we were soon lost in Nottingham trying to find our way to the first school. Luckily we had allowed plenty of time and a cyclist who joined us knew Nottingham well so we all followed her. What a relief! It was fun cycling through the city, but because I was so close to the ground it did feel essential to have people surrounding me as drivers might not see me easily.

We cycled into the primary school. The playground was full of cheering kids with enthusiastic broad smiles. It was heart warming and I looked forward to my first talk there. I was being filmed by both local news channels, and Getty. By the sixth and seventh times we cycled into the school playground for retakes I could feel my genuine surprise and happy face starting to fade. The repetition was simply so the film crew could capture footage from a different angle for what would eventually be on TV for just a few seconds. I had, of course, experienced this during the marathon so it was not unexpected. Nevertheless, each time I re-entered the school I hoped it would be the last time because my smile wasn't quite as genuine as the first time we entered.

Eventually, I was able to get out of the bike and into my chair to go into the school hall. Unfortunately all the kids were already in there waiting; how were we going to keep these small children interested for the length of time it would take us to set up? I think a few of us started to feel the pressure because of this and also, with it being day one, I had a lot of help - possibly too much.

Thankfully this moment passed. Fred was in the hall waiting for me to get strapped in. The video was ready to play and the kid's eyes were glued to it. It gave the background to my journey. As it finished I pressed the control watch and stood up. The kids looked in amazement, there was a robot in their school! I gave my talk, which was very different for these primary school children than the one I gave to older children. When it was question time the hard part was selecting which pupil to pick, with their hands waving frantically in the air. I managed to answer many questions but to demonstrate Fred was not possible. One of the wires had been caught under a leg strap and when I stood up it had wrenched the wire out. Fred no longer worked, and I was stuck in standing position unable to move at all. It had not been a great start and, with the pressure of time and filming, this mistake had been easy to make. Fred does, however, have a manual mode, so with the help of Kate and Charlie I sat down again.

Mick was brilliant at mending things, so he had a job to do that evening. It was not how I hoped the first visit would go and I felt my talk wasn't as good as I had wanted it to be, but I received positive feedback which made me think it had not come across as badly as I feared.

The cycling continued as we headed towards Loughborough. I was getting grief from Henry on every hill we climbed. "What is wrong with you? Why are you so slow? There must be something wrong with you!" I knew exactly how I could shut him up. "Right, tomorrow you are on the spare hand-bike," I said to Henry, smugly. That would teach him.

The lunch break was spent in a lovely pub and everyone, except me, got to enjoy chattering away to each other plus a scrumptious meal. For me, it was just an hour of interviews, both radio and newspapers. In truth, I did have a few minutes in which to eat some lunch but because I also needed a wee, and with a spinal injury everything takes longer, I did not have any time to chill out. The flip-side was it was wonderful to be given so much media attention even though it was only day one, but I felt knackered.

I eventually completed day one in Loughborough, and had a couple more interviews with Getty before I escaped to the Leicester Marriott with Henry and a couple of other friends. After day one of the marathon I had returned buzzing, but after day one of hand-cycling I felt quite low, possibly just exhausted. I was worried how I was going to get through three weeks of this.

I had wanted it to be fun but the day had been so full-on that I rarely had time to enjoy it. I felt it was just a case of being told where to be when, and whom I was speaking to next, with cycling and a school visit in between. Of course all of these things were essential for the fundraising but it was tough. I made sure I ate enough in the evening; pasta was what I needed, and an early night.

The next day was much better. I spent the time cycling in fits of laughter at Henry who was needing to be pushed up almost every steep hill. "Why are you so slow?" I had the pleasure of shouting. Henry swore at me, and carried on struggling.

The first school talk of the day went well, Mick had successfully mended Fred. The secondary school pupils seemed to be engrossed in my story. I got a real buzz seeing some of their reactions. Jo was also cycling with me, as well as Sue, Mum, Dad and other friends. Maisie was at Wendy's most of week one whilst we were local to home so I didn't have to worry about her. I knew she would be having a fantastic time but I missed her.

Dan was still flat out working on his PGCE course, and it was sad that he was unable to be part of the cycle challenge, especially since cycling was a sport he loved. I found that hard. We stopped off at a small café in a town called Anstey where the owner had heard about my cycle challenge, and she refused to charge us. I was once again touched by people's generosity. We were lucky with the weather, the sun was shining and I felt very different from the first day. I was strong, but maybe comparing myself with my slow, weedy, piss-taking friend was making me feel like an elite athlete. Henry was totally shocked how demanding hand-cycling was, and now realised why I had been training religiously all winter in order to be ready to tackle this challenge. Henry confirmed his thoughts: "You are a nutter, cycling that bloody thing; you must be mad!"

We had a second school visit with an incredible welcome. Balloons were up, banners and kids lined up as we arrived. They were clapping and cheering. We had already started to become better organized. I would make sure that I was already strapped into Fred before the pupils came into the hall. I would have a quick stand to readjust to it and prevent any dizziness during my talk. This time I was all ready when the kids entered the hall.

"Oh God, Henry.... I've pissed," I whispered. There was a puddle on the floor. I was at the front of the hall which was now filling up with teenagers. Henry, the genius, passed me a bottle of water which I could conveniently spill down my leg and on the floor. We laughed and shared it with Charlie who didn't know me as well as Henry so he was not as used to my little accidents and embarrassing situations. He was clearly going to see what it is really like living with a spinal cord injury now he was so involved in the cycle challenge.

I was much happier with how my talk went. There were plenty of questions but no one asked why I had a wet patch. There were just as many questions about the marathon, about Fred, and about how I bounced back from such a dark place. As they left the kids started shaking my hand, some asked more questions and thanked me. Staff too were queuing to say goodbye to me and to wish me luck. One lady stopped with a sympathetic look on her face and said: "Thanks. My father-in-law has a brain injury too." Oh dear, maybe my talk wasn't so good after all. It was sad but it also made me laugh, not just for the moment but each time I thought of it. Henry and Jo could, of course, now give me more grief.

We had another seven miles to cycle before the end of the day, and we faced the hassle of packing the bikes up and getting back to the Marriott. Sometimes Mick had to do more than one journey and because he spent much of the time going wrong it could take even longer than expected. The further we were into the cycle challenge the better we got at sorting out these plans.

I had some time with Maisie at the end of day two, and I felt much happier than I did on the first day. My arms were feeling quite good too considering, so I was in a more positive frame of mind. I just had to refrain from thinking of the whole challenge and look no further than the next day, otherwise it was daunting.

The day had finally arrived when I was to join Claire and the team for her cycling challenge. We left the Marriott at 7.30am to travel to a Leicestershire High School and meet other members of the team.

Arriving in plenty of time even with 'Where's Mick' driving, we sorted the technology out and waited in anticipation for the pupils to arrive in the assembly hall. As they filed in, all eyes were on their guest, Claire. There were whispers circulating around the hall until the pupils were settled by a member of staff. Then the hushed silence. Claire was introduced by the Deputy Head and the pupils welcomed her with applause.

Claire showed her video first. This started with her eventing life before her spinal injury. Pupils seemed to grow in their seats as their interest was ignited. The film showed the training and completion of the marathon challenge from the previous year and the media interest involved.

Claire then spoke about how her life had changed in an instant. Total silence and respect was shown for Claire as they listened intently to how she had changed her life since her injury. There was the occasional gasp of disbelief as she told of the daily challenges she faces now. The pupils faces spoke volumes; admiration and respect. Some seemed uncertain that what they were seeing was real. Could anybody faced with such hideous circumstances really be so positive and determined when they worry about such trivial things? You could see that the impact Claire had on some and how it would change their outlook on life. The message 'to never give up' was certainly thought provoking and that was obvious in the questions the youngsters asked Claire at the end. Although the questions, in typical teenage style, were slow initially it soon became evident that we could be there a long time!

The visit was wrapped up as we still had another school to visit, 25 miles to cycle and many more young people to inspire. The team set off enthusiastically and it was great that it was such a big team to accompany Claire on this day. It wasn't too long before the moans started from Henry who had the honour of being in the spare hand cycle! Anyone who thinks it is easy because you are lying down needs to try it...trust me it is HARD! As we made our way around some idyllic villages, the groans were getting louder but then so were the laughs as the insults were flying around and the infamous shouts of 'Car!' from Sue. We eventually all made it to the next school which proved quite traumatic for 'Where's Mick' in the support vehicle. Directions were clearly not his forte, and some of us were apprehensive about the busy roads entering the city centre. Claire delivered her talk at the second school, and then it was time to get back on the bikes to complete the rest of the day's mileage. We had plenty of time! Easier said than done when we set off. The cycling was invigorating even when on the receiving end of the friendly insults and banter that was flying around. We had the perfect weather and it felt great to be part of this. However, the end of the cycle led to many problems. We were in a tiny Leicestershire village with one support vehicle, 10 adults and bikes, no bus route and we had to get to Fosse Park to meet shoppers and pupils from Brockington College who had raised just over £7000 for Claire on her first school visit.

Chaos followed with many suggestions being offered on how we would manage it. Let's just say that wasted a lot of time and with tiredness setting in and deadlines to meet, some suggestions bordered on ridiculous! Somehow we managed it...I won't explain how! But we arrived in time for Claire to meet more young people who she had inspired months before and were desperate to see her again and try out her hand cycle.
Jo Wyeth.

The cycling was undoubtedly physically demanding but the most exhausting aspect about the challenge was having to do two talks a day. It was basically a performance, where my job was to try to inspire the youngsters. It was vital I put 100% into each school. Along with that was local media for each area I travelled through, and I could feel the strain. Even if I was aching, tired and struggling, I needed to come across positive, cheerful and inspiring; that was part of the challenge. It is probably not considered to be tiring by most people, but if you have experienced public speaking then you will probably know how I felt. It required more energy than I had ever anticipated.

The first week was the busiest schedule with three of the evenings spent giving talks, sometimes interviews too. I had some very special moments during that first week. I returned to Ash Field Academy, the first school I went to after the marathon, for children with disabilities. I left the hotel feeling tired and lacking energy. This visit gave me the recharge that I so desperately needed. The children were clearly very excited, and showing them Fred and the hand-bike was a memorable experience. Their faces lit up. One little boy had a go in the hand-bike; he looked absolutely made-up with a grin from ear to ear. Throughout that visit my eyes were full to the brim with tears, along with those of my team who also struggled to hide their emotion. There remained some hilly cycling still to tackle but after visiting Ash Field I felt could take on the world. Their smiles, their joy and their excitement will stay with me for life. They had done some more fundraising by sticking copper coins on very large pieces of paper to make pictures. I was asked to judge it, and it was impossible to do this, the effort they had put in was phenomenal.

Another visit I had that was particularly touching was to Knossington Grange, a therapeutic school for boys that mainstream schools can't manage. We were advised to lock up our bikes and leave nothing out in case it was taken. We arrived in the village in time for lunch at the pub. As I cycled towards it I saw many pasty and serious looking faces. My stomach turned, I thought there must have been an accident. I felt sick. "What's wrong?" I asked. Sue turned around looking devastated and said, "The pub's closed." I was relieved, and told them I thought something drastic had happened. For them this was drastic enough after all the hills we had just climbed.

Everyone at the school was fantastic, and when eight of us were invited for lunch, it was certainly appreciated. Afterwards I gave my talk and demo of Fred. The boys, who I gathered could be unruly at times, didn't make a squeak. They listened to every word and questioned me at the end. Then they kindly presented me with a cheque for £450 which they had raised by doing jobs such as washing cars etc. It was simply fantastic. Some of the lads then cycled with me to Oakham, clearly impressed by the speeds down the hills; we had such a laugh.

One school was a very familiar sight for me. Fifteen years had passed by and a lot had changed in that time, but I was back at my old school, Stamford High. I did an evening interview with Helen Fospero, which parents attended, followed by a talk to the girls the next morning. It was very strange as it all looked pretty much the same, and in some ways, it felt like yesterday when I had sat there as one of the pupils. It really took my mind back to my school days, and all the memories. It was still a lovely school, and I would love Maisie to go there one day.

I was heading into a flatter terrain now, which would do my arms good because they had started to feel the strain from the first week of cycling. Kate helped when she was with me, and Jo contacted a lady who did massage and arranged for her to come out to the hotel. She made me feel revitalised. Again I was shown the kindness of some people when she refused to charge me. I was almost a week into the challenge, but I still wouldn't think further ahead than the next day. I took one day at a time. In fact, when I was cycling I took one hill at a time, bite size pieces rather than the whole.

The Peterborough Marriott, and friend Sam, organised an evening where first I would be interviewed, followed by an auction. Another fantastic £1200 was raised for the Nicholls Spinal Injury Foundation.

After such a long week I found it seriously tough to keep smiling and chatting when really I was desperate for some quiet relaxation time or sleep, but a lady and her partner had travelled three hours to be at the Marriott for my interview and to chat to me. She had been injured about a year previously and knew about my marathon challenge. When I thought back to my first year my heart would sink, the pain and anguish a spinal injured person had to go through is torture, so I could relate to how she was feeling. But I could also share with her how my life had picked up, and how I hoped that hers would too. We had a good chat and if I did help her in any way, then that evening was even more of a success.

Of course I was immensely grateful to Marriott, Sam, and everyone who supported it but I had found it difficult to come across as my lively and usual self. I hope I managed it. As soon as my head hit the pillow I was fast asleep.

Although I hadn't ridden a bike for many years, I still had no hesitation in promising to join Claire during her challenge and not only that, I said I would track down a Raleigh Chopper for the occasion. I had chosen to ride on the first weekend and stayed overnight at the hotel, before making my way down to the bank in Peterborough where Claire was giving some interviews before the cycling began for the day. The day started off pretty miserably, and the schedule was soon disrupted when torrential rain forced us to abandon the plan to leave Peterborough centre on our bikes. Instead we headed in our cars to the nearby village to Claire's starting point.

When we arrived in the village the couple in the vehicle in front got out, both dressed from head-to-toe in the correct lycra cycling gear and then lifted down their posh road bikes using one finger ... here I was, dressed in bright orange trousers, a fluorescent yellow shirt and a visor with a mop of ginger hair, in the form of a wig, trying unsuccessfully to lift a Raleigh Chopper from the car. What had I let myself in for?

We set off and the first 100 yards was no problem. I soon realised my legs were going four times as quick as everyone else's yet I was going twice as slow. This was going to be a long, long day. Luckily we had regular stops and I've still no idea whether this was for genuine drink breaks or just to give
me time to get back into the same county as all the others! We eventually stopped for lunch at a lovely village pub and after about 13 miles on that Chopper I was glad for the break.

Towards the end of lunch I got a bit of unexpected news as Claire asked Mick to get the spare hand-cycle from the trailer as 'Stuart was going to be using it this afternoon!' I had mixed feelings, one was relief that there would be no more peddling like an idiot, but then again, I had never been in the hand-cycle before and wasn't certain I would be strong enough to keep up. However, I wasn't going to turn down the challenge and I had seen Claire all morning, albeit from a good distance behind, and she made it look so easy. Bring it on!

After a quick run through of the gears we set off and everything was perfect for the first 20 yards, until I had to turn the corner ... for some reason I had got it into my head that this should be done with my legs.

Why? If that were the case, Claire would only be able to travel in straight lines! My initial observation that hand-cycling looks fairly easy was spot on. It does look easy. However, it's not until you have a go yourself that you realise just how hard it actually is. Flat roads are pretty much what I expected, not easy but manageable, but any slight incline and my arms were soon aching and quickly tired and there was no way I could keep up with Claire. The only consolation was that I wasn't last anymore as the hand-cycles are so low that it is best a cyclist stays behind you for protection from the traffic. There were a couple of steep hills that if I hadn't got a push from someone I think I wouldn't have made it.

We all joined up near Huntingdon town centre and we were to cycle down together into the pedestrian area of the town where the cameras were waiting to film Claire's arrival. This was a great experience as there were many people about on a Saturday afternoon lining both sides of the street. We then made our way back to the support vehicle, and when I reached the car park and stopped beside Claire she gave me that fantastic smile and a high five. Bloody hell, I felt so proud.

I had completed around 11 miles on the hand-cycle and was shattered ... Claire was doing 25 miles a day for over three weeks, plus the school visits and the interviews and some evening talks. Just looking at her schedule made me feel exhausted. Without any doubt, unless you have experienced the hand-cycle for yourself you cannot fully appreciate what Claire has actually achieved. Truly Amazing. Truly Inspirational.

No doubt this was just a tiny part of the amazing challenge but what an honour and privilege it was to be involved. A day that will live with me forever.
Stuart Hall.

I had a good variety of schools to visit. The difference between primary and secondary was vast. I always had lots of questions from both but primary school kids would ask funny things. "If I got a chain saw and cut your leg off would you feel that?" "Are any of your horses in burgers?" The kids would ask anything.

I enjoyed the primary schools but felt my story was making more of an impression on secondary school pupils as they understood the impact of my accident. I always found it boosted my energy when I received messages from the pupils and they told me how much I had inspired them. It felt amazing that I could leave the schools having given a strong message, and I would never have thought this was possible but through the comments I had received I had gained confidence. If I could have a positive influence on a few children in a school then it was well worth my time. Equally important was that they were raising money so that one day paralysed people will be walking again.

Throughout the whole challenge the spare bike was used, although not by me, because my new Quickie hand-bike didn't have any problems, but plenty of friends had the opportunity to have a go at hand-cycling. I took great pleasure in racing them; most of them were fit men who were mortified at being beaten by a paralysed female. Not until they got in the hand-cycle to try it did they realise why I was so steady up-hill, and it was a fantastic feeling for me to have someone behind for a change.

We had a rota of people to help with the school visits, cycling, and driving. Mick did much of the driving but frequently in the wrong direction. At one stage he was totally lost in Hitchin but when we asked where he was he simply replied, 'Near a river'. None of us knew the area so we were unsure how to direct him back to us. We couldn't believe our luck when a woman who came to cycle with us knew the area inside out, and somehow managed to direct 'Where's Mick' back to us. I felt total relief to see him as it seemed that we were close to sending a search party. We did have a Sat-Nav but he still got lost. I later heard him on the phone, "Sorry, I can't make it," he said. "I am on a cycle ride from Brighton to London." The whole team looked at each other in disbelief. We couldn't help but love him being a part of the cycling team, and he certainly enjoyed his journey with us. He provided us with laughs on so many occasions.

Very early on in the planning stages of the cycle ride I offered myself to Claire for at least five days of the three weeks. Once the rough route was confirmed to be coming through my area I booked days off work and offered to be a mounted assistant / trailer driver / fetch and carry boy. Luckily for me Claire accepted my offer and I was on the team.

On the bike ride there were lots of laughs and giggles, bumpy roads and hills and some very fast downhill races! It turns out that a hand-cycle is incredibly slow up hill, literally walking pace but downhill... Bloody hell she was like a rocket! Now I'm relatively young, tall, fit and a keen cyclist and I love nothing more than being in top gear and trying to top 30 miles per hour downhill but on every single downhill stretch I had to get a good 100 yards ahead of Claire to have any chance of being able to keep up with her! Basically I had 5 days of racing around the countryside, going steady up hill and on the flat and then absolutely blasting it downhill.... Great fun!

Apart from that, and actually getting to talk to Claire as we hadn't properly met before, the most amazing thing was watching and listening to her talk to the school kids, a major part of the challenge. To my knowledge Claire isn't a trained public speaker or teacher but my god can she get a group of kids to hang on to every word! Whether they were primary or secondary, she has the ability to pass on her message to any audience, perfectly adjusting her delivery as required, and all that was on top of hand-cycling!

One day I had the opportunity to have a go in Claire's spare hand-bike. Now I thought I was being clever by picking the straightest, flattest and probably easiest day of the week, as I knew the hand-cycle would be hard after seeing others struggle, but I was not prepared for it whatsoever. Each hill we came to I was completely left for dust and there was no way I could keep up. I think for the rest of the week I tried to make excuses as to why the bike I was using was heavier, slower, and creakier than Claire's and that's why she was so fast.
Michael Rogers.

Dan managed to escape from his studies for a day. It was a great sight for me to see him cycling with Maisie on the back of his bike. We didn't have a school visit because it was a weekend which meant a more relaxed day.

Maisie was impeccably behaved on the challenge. She spent time in the schools, in the support vehicle or playing outside. In the evenings we would try to find time to get her in the swimming pool at the hotel which she enjoyed. She was always excited moving to a new hotel, and I loved having her with me. Mum also stayed each night once we were in week two and further from home.

The final week was the hardest. I had picked up a nasty cold and I was struggling to continue. In a normal situation I would have taken a couple of easier days to fight it off, but I was having to go out each day and push myself physically and also do a lot of speaking, so it got worse. My spinal injury makes coughing difficult and my breathing is not as strong, so a cold really knocks the stuffing out of me. I dosed up on painkillers, tried to make sure all the schools had a microphone, and I carried on. It was not enjoyable and I longed to see the finish.

I had about six days left and the cold was so bad that I couldn't manage as much cycling as usual, so I did a shorter day and added the lost miles to the last few days. I had needed to have an easier day so as to give myself some chance of fighting it off. It did help as the next day I felt slightly better.

I had a visit to Eton College which was planned much later than the rest. It was the most stunning of schools as I had expected, and the boys looked exceptionally smart in their tail coats. It was filmed by Getty and being in such a prestigious school made me a bit more nervous although I knew it shouldn't really. The boy's faces looked as if they were interested, but funnily enough I got asked the fewest number of questions by Eton pupils than by any of the other schools. I encouraged them to ask anything they liked and I knew that often the first question took a while. I did get about five in the end but they didn't seem as confident as I thought they would be. They were polite and thanked me on their way out.

I'd really enjoyed visiting such a huge range of schools, and there was not one I didn't get a buzz from, even when I felt ill.

Now that they had become used to cycling each day, my arms had passed through the sore stage and felt stronger than ever. After a school visit, I relished the freedom and fresh air that I got from hand-cycling. I was always aiming to get my personal best speed down the hills, and I saw a lovely steep hill approaching. "Steady down here," Dad shouted. To anyone else they would have thought he was worried about me losing control but I knew different. Dad was worried but today it wasn't about my safety, it was the fact that he knew he wasn't going to be able to keep up and we were both competitive. I clocked my best speed of 48mph and, being close to the ground, it felt even faster; it was exhilarating.

I had only one day off cycling during the three week challenge, and it was spent at Salisbury Racecourse. We had permission to collect for the charities, and I had an interview in the paddock. I used Fred to stand at the exit gate where we collected donations. It was evident that we got more donations when I was standing tall in Fred so I stayed there for a long time. Sitting down just didn't have the same effect. We were happy to find we had raised over £800.

By now seven able bodied men had attempted hand-cycling with me, and had failed to beat me. That was before I took on a race against double Olympic rowing gold medalist Tom James. Tom was the boyfriend of someone Mum knew, and he very kindly said he would join me in Richmond Park. He jumped into the spare hand-bike and right from the start I could see that this was going to be a true challenge. We chose a quiet road to have our race and we lined up at the start point. I pushed myself to the limit but Tom was a foot in front all the way. I couldn't quite catch him but I enjoyed trying. It was great to be able to tell the seven other men that there was obviously nothing wrong with the spare hand-bike because Tom had won in it. They had tried to blame the bike when they were slower than me.

I was sitting in the hotel looking at the agenda for the last day with a smile on my face. I had almost made it, after months of planning, training and three demanding weeks. I just had to survive the London traffic, something I anticipated would be quite terrifying, low down on a hand-bike. Becca and Dave from Freud had organised it all exceptionally well and we even had two experienced London cyclists to help us get through the city safely. We would not have to worry about directions at all.

An early start was pretty much normal now as I usually had to be at a school quite early and the last day was no exception. We drove across London to the school in Chelsea to do my final talk. It was surprising that I still got nervous after 25 talks and countless media interviews but this was essential because these nerves kept my talks lively; each as if it were my first. This one was extra special, knowing it was the last talk for a while, and we had a fantastic send off from the school.

Daybreak presenters and friends Dan Lobb and Helen Fospero joined me. Dan was roped into cycling my spare hand-bike which was a new experience for him. He was lucky that there were not many hills in central London. In total there were 12 of us cycling, and it was a perfect end to the challenge. The route was brilliant, passing several of London's landmarks for photo opportunities. We stopped outside the Royal Albert Hall, 10 Downing Street, and Trafalgar Square where

Melanie C joined us. I had asked her after meeting her at Tesco Mum of the Year, and I couldn't believe it when she said she was up for it. She was so easy to chat to, and such a genuine and kind person. I was delighted that she was part of the final day; I never thought I would be cycling through the centre of London with Sporty Spice.

After the usual time taken for photo shoots and filming, we were almost there. The finish line was less than a mile away; the London Eye didn't look far away at all. We pulled over and waited whilst Becca and Dave checked that everything was in place for me to finish. I was given the go ahead to do the last part of the cycle. I stripped off so I had the branded top on ready for the interviews, but without a jacket I felt a little cold. I made sure I cycled quickly to stay as warm as I possibly could.

By the London Eye was a large gathering of people. Once again the media lined up behind the finishing line that had been put up by Becca. Friends and family were there too, as well as small clusters of school kids from a few of the schools I had visited. Jo had managed to bring a group from Brockington College, St Lukes special school had selected a few to be there, and a primary school from Didcot had a school outing. It was fantastic to see them all again in London; they were holding banners which they had made to congratulate me.

Gary Lineker, Julie Etchingham, Gaby Roslin, and Rav Wilding were among the many celebrities who joined me at the finish. It was very generous of them to give up their time and to help raise awareness of spinal injuries. I was flanked by all this support for the last few yards that I cycled. I came to a stand still and Maisie ran over and gave me the best hug in the world; I shall treasure moments like that all my life. Sadly for me, Dan wasn't able to get away from college, and it was no doubt particularly tough for him too, but it wouldn't be long before he was qualified and his hard work and commitment would have been worth it.

The cycle challenge raised over £85,000 for the charities. This, combined with the hundreds of children I had spoken to on the journey, made it a huge success. This was not just about me; everyone who had given up their time to help had made this possible. Not only would it not have been possible without the help of others, it would not have been a fraction of the fun it had been either. My family, my friends, and others who made me laugh or humbled me, no matter how exhausted I felt, all of them kept me going.

On the last night I was treated to a night at the luxury Marriott County Hall hotel, which was located next to the London Eye on the banks of the Thames. They put on the perfect celebration, with champagne flowing and scrumptious food for all of us. The room was gorgeous and there was even a present for Maisie left in there, a beautiful teddy bear.

When I was able to stop and think about the whole challenge, I was thrilled with how it had gone. If people compared it with the marathon then they might not think that it went as well because it hadn't raised as much, but £85,000 was raised, and this was something I was still extremely proud of. I had also witnessed some of the children's faces as they watched me walk in Fred, or sat in my handbike and had their photo taken; some of their smiles could light up the world. This is what made this cycle challenge so immensely rewarding and so very special in its own way!

It had felt like a never-ending challenge at times, but it was also crammed full of laughs and fun with a wonderful group of people. I was definitely ready to finish, and excited about returning home to see Dan and to get back into another routine.

So what is next?

13

Only two days after I had delivered my last school talk I was feeling the nerves all over again; I was about to speak to 500 women at a local luncheon to which I had been invited as the guest speaker. This was all arranged before I had even confirmed the cycle challenge dates, otherwise I might have chosen to have an easier week. Now it was one of the last things I felt like doing but, as usual, once I was there I thoroughly enjoyed the afternoon. I felt lucky to be able to make a living from these speaking events; they never fail but to give me the adrenaline rush I need. They also fit in incredibly well with bringing up Maisie and the fundraising. I still found it very hard to believe that something I would once have hated was now a big part of my life.

The question I am most frequently asked is: "What are you going to do next?" I had given this much thought after the cycle challenge. Without the school visits the cycling would have not raised anywhere the £85,000 we actually did, so I felt another sporting event was not perhaps the best thing for me to do at the moment. Before the marathon I would have been thrilled to raise £10,000 but after two incredible fundraising challenges, it would now feel like I had not achieved what I wanted to.

Because my family is the most important aspect of my life, I could not do a sport where I had to be away training much of the time. So, for now, I decided that I would continue to raise money by visiting schools plus organising a couple of social events as I had in the past.

I was definitely going to enjoy hand-cycling throughout the summer. It is a fantastic sport that I can do with friends and family and even incorporate pub stops en-route. It was nigh on impossible not to be inspired by the London Paralympics, the athletes demonstrated that despite having a disability they had more ability than many people. 'Maybe I could be at Rio,' I thought. I had been in touch with British Cycling and considered trying racing. For a few months I was fighting with myself about the idea of giving it a go or keeping it as a hobby. I have always been passionate about sport and I am competitive by nature so it did feel a very attractive option. Whether I would be fast enough would be another thing, but there was one thing for certain, I could never be a winner without serious training and dedication. I was a 33 year-old mum now. Ten years ago I would have been willing to train for hours a day, like I was with my eventing. When I thought about it I knew I could not put in the commitment it would need. If it came to a choice between watching Maisie in a school play or a very important race my priority would certainly be with Maisie. Life before the accident was largely consumed by a sport, which of course I loved. The knocks and disappointments have been hard to take and I definitely think my sporting experience helped me to tackle my life changing accident more positively. To compete in a sport at the top level and be successful does mean you have to put it first much of the time and I did not want to go back to that. I had developed what I thought was a perfect balance between my life, my family, fundraising, sport and work. Why change this? I also got a huge sense of achievement from raising money to help to find a cure for paralysis. Without a shadow of doubt, I live every day in the hope that one day in the future I shall witness the recovery of spinal injured people. Nothing will give me greater satisfaction. To me, that would be far better than winning any amount of gold medals, for it will be transforming thousands of people's lives all over the world.

The marathon and cycle challenges had opened many doors for me, and I have taken advantage of as many opportunities as possible. I was invited to speak for the Zionist Federation at a science week. The Zionist Federation demonstrates some of the excellent work Israel is doing, and I took Fred along to show what Amit had invented. Not many months later they invited my family and me over to Israel. I contacted ReWalk and arranged to meet the ReWalk team over there. It was mainly a family holiday with a little bit of work integrated into what was a brilliant week.

I saw how far they had come with developing the ReWalk suit but it also made me realise just how many more improvements they intended to make. They wanted my feedback as one of their first users, and we discussed all the things that could make Fred even better. They are working on making it more compact and lighter, as well as possibly being able to have different length steps.

We had a lovely dinner at Amit's house with his family, and it was a pleasure to spend some time with the man who had invented and built the remarkable device that enabled me to walk the London Marathon. It made me appreciate Fred even more. Amit had spent years designing the ReWalk suit that has changed my life and led me to doing things I never thought I would.

Nothing gave me more pleasure than watching Maisie play in the sea and on the beach. I remembered when I was at Project Walk, only three months after my accident, I could barely sit on the beach to see people playing in the sea and walking across the sand. I would sit there with my head full of negative self-destructive thoughts. Now, here I was, sitting on the beach admiring our own little girl as she played in the sea. Since my injured body, with a little help from Dan, had produced a miracle, I became happy and confident. I was no longer self-conscious; I never thought this would be possible.

We had all had a truly wonderful week. The return journey was somewhat stressful. Maisie had started to show early signs of chicken pox, although she didn't seem to be unwell; I knew this could mean we'd be unable to fly. I was relieved when we had boarded the plane without any hassle. I had felt a bit dodgy myself for the past twelve hours and if I knew I had a tummy bug I wouldn't have dared to get on the flight.

We had been in the air for about an hour when I became aware of an unpleasant aroma. I thought Maisie had done a poo but I checked her nappy and she was fine. Maybe it was the baby behind me? I reached to get Maisie a toy and as I moved the smell was significantly worse. I looked over to Mum in horror. "I have shat," I whispered. "What the hell am I going to do?" I asked.

Of course there was nothing I could do, except sit very still and wait another four hours to land, and then another two until I got home. An upset tummy whilst on a flight could mortify able-bodied people but at least they have the loo on the plane in which to take refuge. For me this was far too tiny, I couldn't get in there if I tried and, worse, if I attempted to move I was worried I would stink the whole plane out. "I think she has done a poo," said the four-year-old girl in front, looking at Maisie. I made out I would change her nappy.

This flight was the longest four hours one could ever experience. I looked at my watch more often than I looked at the map whilst walking the marathon. The Duty Free trolley passed through so I purchased some lovely expensive Jean-Paul Gaultier perfume, hoping that it would help, as I sprayed it all over myself every half hour. It may have appeared a strange thing to do but it was essential. Every ten minutes or so I would ask

Mum and Dan if they could smell me, which they insisted they couldn't but I felt so paranoid. This was a total nightmare, thank goodness this was six and a half years after my accident and not in the first year. I certainly would not have coped then; I would have tried to jump out of the plane except I couldn't jump. I didn't eat or drink a thing on the flight even though I felt like I was dying of thirst. I just sat there like a statue, which made entertaining two year old Maisie very difficult.

It was such a relief to arrive home. The next two days were spent in the shower or waiting to go in the shower again.

Of course, my life still has its difficulties due to my spinal cord injury; this is something that hasn't changed. I cannot even go away on holiday and leave it behind, it comes with me everywhere and causes me trouble wherever I am, and I still have the usual stress that most people have, that is life. It had been a tough year for Dan. He had a particularly demanding course where he was getting little sleep but I am proud he stuck at it. He has now qualified as a science teacher. We will soon be moving into our own new house, much to the relief of my parents, and at the time of writing Dan is starting his new job.

I still have moments where I may be fed up or annoyed about something minor, like anyone, but I no longer dwell on my injury. It has made me who I am and it has given me the opportunities I have had. I know I have been lucky to have the incredible support and boundless love from my family and friends, but I also know that you have to make your own luck.

In the early days I spent hours thinking about and focusing on the things I had lost and what I couldn't do. I was angry, I was sad and I sometimes wallowed in self pity. Why had this happened to me? I realised that I had to start to think about everything I could do and what I still had. This didn't happen overnight, it took time and every ounce of strength I had in me. I had to dig deep. This was my biggest challenge, bigger than I had ever faced. Gradually the good days started to outweigh the bad days and I started to see the light at the end of the tunnel. The doors that were slammed in my face started to spring open for me, one by one. I made sure that I explored what was on the other side of these doors, and life started to pick up. I soon discovered there was a whole big new world out there and it was down to me to make the most of my life. I have had the chance to have two lives, that is lucky. I am the same person but my life now is very different from the one prior to my accident; the truth is, it really is better.

I have made some special friends; I have lost some not so special friends since my accident. I wouldn't turn back the time – I now look forward to the future.

So what lies in the future?

I decided to write this book myself after considering a ghost-writer. It has been tougher than I anticipated, and the memories it has brought back have made me both sob and laugh, sometimes both at the same time. I felt no one could write it for me because only I can describe how I felt during those bleak days, and explain what I have experienced. I've had no experience with writing, and the process was daunting. I chose to hand write it all because the moment I picked up the pen my feelings and thoughts came flooding out. I wrote on the days when Wendy had Maisie so I had complete peace. In two months I had written it, quicker than I expected. Dan typed it up as I completed each chapter. I then had a team of friends helping me by editing and proofreading. I faced the decision of whether I should try to get a publisher or self publish. In the end I decided to go ahead and do it myself. I took the book on as one of my challenges, and I hope it helps to raise more vital funds required in order for The Nicholls Foundation to push on towards the cure. Once again, I have enjoyed doing something that I previously would never have contemplated, I hope you have enjoyed reading my story as much as I did writing it.

I am truly proud to be a patron of the Nicholls Spinal Injury Foundation. I shall continue to do what I can to raise money for them and awareness of spinal injuries. The work the Nicholls Foundation is doing is truly breathtaking. I firmly believe that the cure for paralysis is not too far away. It will improve the lives of thousands and thousands of people. I am living a happy life but I know from first-hand experience of all the complications and struggles that everyone with a spinal injury faces. Imagine not being able to feed yourself, scratch an itch, hug your child, walk, run; I saw all of this in hospital. Now imagine what a difference the work that the charity is doing could make to these people's lives.

I now have new dreams. Dreams that I know will come true. I will walk the London marathon again, one day, without Fred. I don't doubt that I shall 'find my feet' for real.

The Nicholls Spinal Injury Foundation needs vital funds to keep pushing on with the promising work they are doing. Thank you so much for supporting the charity by purchasing my book. Every penny counts.

To donate to the Nicholls Spinal Injury Foundation please visit:

www.justgiving.com/clairesupportsNF/

Or text LEGS60 £ (any amount between £1–£10) to 70070

WEBSITES

www.get-claire-walking.co.uk

www.claireschallenge.co.uk

www.nichollsfoundation.org.uk

www.matthampson.co.uk

The Nicholls Spinal Injury Foundation Story

On December 30th 2003, my son Daniel dived into a wave on Bondi Beach. A hidden sandbank lay beneath the water and when Dan hit it, he broke his neck. Dan was nineteen at the time and just five weeks into his gap year. He was left paralysed from the arms down with very little movement in his hands.

I flew out to Australia to find my son in this totally bleak, helpless and – according to the doctors – hopeless condition. Whilst in the hospital in Australia I met another young, newly paralysed man whose parents, unable to face their son's condition, left him to a life in care. Apparently this was not uncommon. I was stunned, and unwilling to accept what future seemed to lie in store for these young men. So I made a promise to Dan that I would get him back on his feet one day.

My background was as an executive chef and business director in the food and beverage industry. I knew my connections from the industry would be willing to help, so I began fundraising. My friends rallied to help me without a second thought, helping me create a cookbook, Off Duty, a collection of home and family inspired recipes from some of the world's most celebrated chefs. Against the advice of leading literary agent Ed Victor, who is also a personal friend, I chose to self publish. Against the odds, Harper Collins agreed to distribute the book for free, because the CEO's brother-in-law had recently been paralysed. I dubbed this the ripple effect, a phenomenon that has ever since been central to the way charity operates and to its success.

Once we had raised almost half a million pounds, I began to look for a charity to give the money to. On closer inspection, I found that admin costs ranged from 40-60%. I also found that very few funded scientific research, focusing instead on palliative care. I strongly believed that a cure would come through science, despite the scepticism of the medical community. I was also

257

unwilling to let such a large portion of the money we had raised go towards paying costs. With my background as a business director, I knew it was possible to operate at a lower cost ratio. And so in 2005, The Nicholls Spinal Injury Foundation came about, focused on funding a cure for spinal injury and maintaining admin costs of 10% or below.

The charity operated initially as a close network of friends with a shared purpose. Then the search for a beneficiary began. Every time I read the news for the latest information on spinal injuries one name kept popping up. Professor Geoffrey Raisman continued to appear in the headlines, but not in the way a parent looking for hope wanted: every claim of success made was dismissed by the professor as inaccurate and misleading. Then The Times ran a seven-page article on Geoffrey Raisman, calling him The Miracle Worker. I was intrigued, and set out to meet Professor Raisman. But I was convinced the professor wasn't the man I wished to fund.

To my surprise, Professor Raisman was in no way a pessimist about a cure for spinal injury; he just didn't believe one had been found yet. He explained to me the little-known fact that almost half of paralysed patients will walk again without any intervention in the spinal cord, and how these facts are sometimes peddled as evidence of some pretended cure.

Professor Raisman's own work is based on using stem cells – which form the only regenerative part of the central nervous system – to re-establish pathways that can lead damaged nerve fibres to regenerate to their original targets.

The professor was profoundly hopeful that spinal cord repair was possible, but he also knew great caution had to be exercised in making claims to people who had experienced one of the most devastating experiences a person can go through.

His clear and unassailable reasoning, his categorical assertion that there would be a cure, changed my mind, and convinced me the professor was indeed the man I wanted the charity to fund. The partnership was formed and to date all grants TNSIF has made have been to Geoff Raisman and, since the start of 2013, to his colleague and research partner, Dr. Pawel Tabakov, a surgeon at The Polish Academy of Sciences in Wroclaw.

In 2007 TNSIF held its first Celebrity Golf Day. It was a fantastic success and the model has been repeated annually since, raising over £750,000, with funds also coming in via the charity's many patrons. Today, TNSIF has given away over £2 million whilst maintaining a 10% cost ratio.

In 2012, I met Claire through a mutual friend. Our shared conviction that there would be a cure for spinal injuries led to an immediate bond and Claire offered her support to TNSIF. She has worked tirelessly ever since, becoming one of the charity's most prolific fundraisers. As recounted in these pages, despite being unable to take a step in 2011, Claire has since raised thousands of pounds for TNSIF through walks, cycle rides and school talks.

It is not just Claire's dedication to fundraising that I value greatly. Her warmth and positivity, and the way she manages to have a sense of humour about her condition, have helped her become a role model for people dealing with adversity. And she has used her high profile in the press and on social media to champion the foundation's single-minded message: One day there will be a cure for spinal paralysis.